CULTURES OF THE WORLD

TAHITI

Roseline NgCheong-Lum

MARSHALL CAVENDISH
New York • London • Sydney

Reference edition published 1997 by
Marshall Cavendish Corporation
99 White Plains Road
Tarrytown
New York 10591

© Times Editions Pte Ltd 1997

Originated and designed by
Times Books International, an imprint of
Times Editions Pte Ltd

Printed in Singapore

Library of Congress Cataloging-in-Publication Data:
NgCheong-Lum, Roseline.
    Tahiti / Roseline NgCheong-Lum.
      p. cm.—(Cultures of the World)
    Contents: Includes bibliographical references and index.
    Summary: Discusses the geography, history, government,
economy, people, and culture of the largest island in French
Polynesia.
    ISBN 0-7614-0682-4 (lib. bdg. : alk. paper)
    1. Tahiti—Juvenile literature. [1. Tahiti.]
I. Title. II. Series.
DU870.C46 1997
919.62'11—dc21   96–40213
                        CIP
                        AC

INTRODUCTION

SET IN THE HEART of the Pacific Ocean, Tahiti is a land of contrasts. Tall, craggy mountains drop down abruptly to beaches of white sand lapped by gentle waves. While Papeete, the capital, is cosmopolitan and bustling with activity, the peninsula that makes up the eastern part of the island is wild and undeveloped.

Since the day of its discovery by Europeans, Tahiti has been praised as a blessed island whose name is almost synonymous with paradise. The word conjures up images of sun-drenched beaches, lazy days, and a happy people full of lust for life. However, Tahiti's history is one of domination by chiefs and European colonizers. Having endured more than a century of French rule, the population is now ready to take charge of its own destiny. This book, part of the *Cultures of the World* series, studies the dilemma facing the Tahitians and their efforts to come to terms with their opposing cultural heritages.

CONTENTS

A Tahitian relaxes outside his colorful home.

CONTENTS

Hand-made hats and a beautiful quilt in the traditional Tahitian style.

GEOGRAPHY

THE NAME "TAHITI" IS USED to refer to the island of Tahiti as well as to the whole of French Polynesia. This territory in the Pacific Ocean forms part of the "Polynesian triangle," which includes Hawaii in the north, Easter Island in the east and New Zealand in the southwest.

French Polynesia is spread over a total area of 1,545,000 square miles (4,001,550 square km), about half the size of the U. S. mainland. It is made up of 118 islands, which have a combined land area of only 1,544 square miles (4,000 sq. km). These islands are divided into five archipelagos: the Society Islands, Austral Islands, Tuamotu Islands, Gambier Islands, and the Marquesas. The Society Islands are further divided into the Windward Islands and Leeward Islands. Located in the Windward group, the largest island in French Polynesia is Tahiti, where most of the population lives. Tahiti is also the commercial, cultural, and social center of French Polynesia. Other important islands are Moorea, Huahine, and Raiatea.

The word "Polynesia" is made up of two Greek words, poly *and* nesos, *which mean "many islands."*

Left: **Playing volleyball on a beach of black volcanic sand.**

Opposite: **Lush tropical vegetation and beautiful waterfalls characterize Tahiti's mountainous interior.**

THE ISLAND OF TAHITI

Tahiti has only one lake, Lake Vaihiria, perched at an altitude of 1,500 feet (457 m). It is known for its huge eels endowed with large, ear-like fins. According to legend, the first eel crawled across the mountains from a pool in Arue on the northern coast. Feeling lonely, the eel married a beautiful maiden. The present-day inhabitants are supposed to be the descendants of this incongruous couple.

Although Tahiti is the largest island in French Polynesia, it is only about one-third the size of Rhode Island. However, its area of 402 square miles (1,041 square km) accounts for about one-quarter of the total land area of French Polynesia. It is also the highest island, at 7,337 feet (2,235 m).

The islands of French Polynesia are of two types: volcanic islands, also called high islands, and coral islands, also called atolls. Tahiti is a high island ringed by a coral reef. It is shaped like an hourglass lying more or less horizontal. The larger section of the hourglass, Tahiti Nui (Big Tahiti), takes up the western side of the island. Papeete ("pah-pay-AY-tay"), the capital, is located on the northwest coast of Tahiti Nui. Most activity is concentrated in the town and the area surrounding it. The airport of Faaa ("fah-AH-ah") is about 4 miles (6.4 km) from Papeete.

The smaller part of Tahiti is a peninsula called Tahiti Iti (Small Tahiti) or Taiarapu. It is mostly undeveloped, and there is no road going all the way around it. The narrow neck of the hourglass is called Taravao, and it acts as a refueling center for people traveling around Tahiti.

Like Hawaii's Maui, Tahiti was formed by two ancient volcanoes joined at the isthmus of Taravao. The centers of both parts of Tahiti are mountainous and craggy. Steep slopes crossed by deep ravines descend to the coastal plain. Waterfalls are a common sight; Vaimahuta, near Tiarei in the northeast, is one of the most beautiful. Rainbows form above the waterfalls as the sun's rays filter through the droplets of water. In fact, the islanders call their country Tahiti-nui-te-vai-uri-rau, which means "Great Tahiti of the many-colored waters."

The coastal plain varies in width from a few feet (around 1 m) to over a mile (1.6 km) at its widest in the north at Pirae and the south at Papara. Only the coastal plain is inhabited.

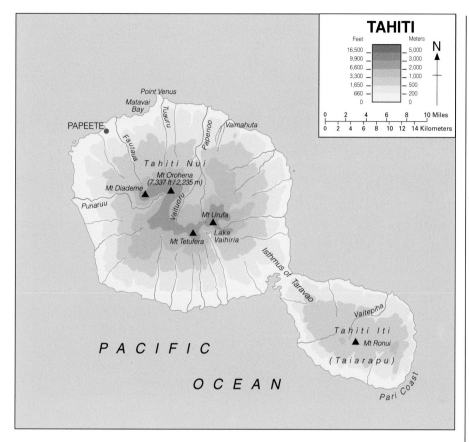

TAHITI

Feet		Meters
16,500		5,000
9,900		3,000
6,600		2,000
3,300		1,000
1,650		500
660		200
0		0

N

0   2   4   6   8   10 Miles
0   2   4   6   8   10   12   14 Kilometers

Point Venus
Matavai Bay
PAPEETE
Tuauru
Papenoo
Vaimahuta
Faataua
Tahiti Nui
Mt Orohena (7,337 ft / 2,235 m)
Mt Diademe
Punaruu
Vaituoru
Mt Urufa
Lake Vaihiria
Mt Tetufera
Isthmus of Taravao
Vaitepiha
Tahiti Iti
Mt Ronui
(Taiarapu)
Pari Coast

PACIFIC

OCEAN

Next to Matavai Bay is Point Venus, so named because Captain Cook observed the transit of the planet Venus across the sun from this point in 1769.

The northeastern coast is rugged and rocky because there is no barrier reef. Waves ride high, pounding the shore with intensity. Villages lie in a narrow strip between the mountains and the ocean. The Pari Coast, at the southeastern tip of the peninsula, has spectacular cliffs dropping nearly 1,000 feet (305 meters) down to the ocean. The south coast, on the other hand, is protected by a reef, and the sandy beaches are gently lapped by the waves. The coastal plain is broad and supports large gardens and coconut groves. All around Tahiti, the depth of the lagoon between the reef and the island varies from 25 feet (7.6 m) to 100 feet (30.5 m).

The coastline is cut here and there by deep bays. Matavai Bay is where most of the early explorers landed. All ships moored in Matavai Bay until the 1820s, when the better protected harbor of Papeete became more popular.

BIRTH OF AN ATOLL

Islands in the ocean are formed by underwater volcanic eruptions. As the volcano explodes, magma is pushed up above sea level, and an island emerges. At first, it is shaped like a cone. After the mass has cooled down, rains slowly erode the land, and valleys and mountains are carved out of the cone. Once this phase is over, the island gradually becomes surrounded by a ring of coral.

The action of the rain over several million years causes the island to slowly erode away. At the same time, the coral reef grows higher and higher, rising to about 3–7 feet (0.9–2.1 m) above sea level. Vegetation starts to grow on this ring, and the edges become beaches. As the ring is not of the same height throughout, the parts that jut out of the sea become coral islands. These are called *motu* ("moh-TOO") in Tahitian. When the last volcanic peak of the first island is completely submerged by the sea, leaving only the ring of coral islands surrounding a lagoon, an atoll is born.

"Closed" atolls have no break in the reef. The only way water is exchanged between the ocean and the lagoon is through shallow channels called *hoa* ("HOH-ah"). "Open" atolls can have one or more breaks in the reef, promoting greater exchange of water and marine species between the ocean and the lagoon. Makatea, in the Tuamotu archipelago, is the only "raised" atoll in French Polynesia. The reef that turned into the island was wider and higher, thus forming a plateau with no lagoon.

PEAKS AND RIVERS

The centers of Tahiti Nui and Tahiti Iti are made up of several tall peaks surrounding a deep depression. The depression, called a caldera, is the former crater of the volcano whose explosion led to the formation of the island. The tallest mountain on Tahiti Nui is Mount Orohena. Its rounded summit rises up to 7,337 feet (2,235 m). Tahiti Iti's tallest peak is Mount Roniu at 3,696 feet (1,126 m). Altogether there are eight mountains on the island of Tahiti. One of the most intriguing outcrops is Mount Diademe, a thin rectangular blade of basalt that rises to 3,963 feet (1,207 m).

There are more than 100 rivers and streams all over Tahiti. The longest river is Papenoo, which originates from the northern side of the caldera of Tahiti Nui. At its source, where it is spanned by the longest bridge in Tahiti, it is called Vaituoru. It then becomes Papenoo and travels 15 miles (24 km) through the Papenoo Valley down to the sea. On its way it is joined by several other rivers and divides into two before reaching the sea. The widest and fast-flowing river in Tahiti is the Vaitepiha on the peninsula.

Tahiti's steep mountains and valleys are very scenic, but they make the interior of the island unsuitable for habitation and agriculture.

PAPEETE

Tahiti's capital takes its name from the Papeete River, which used to flow nearby. Meaning "water basket," Papeete was nothing but a swamp until Rev. James Crook, an English missionary, settled on a hill overlooking the swamp in 1818. The missionaries of the London Missionary Society soon followed suit, and the town started its unstoppable growth. Its excellent harbor made it a place of trade and a favorite port of call for whalers. After Tahiti was made a French colony in 1880, Papeete became the seat of the governor.

The town now extends over 25 miles (40 km) from Paea in the west to Mahina in the north. The districts of Papenoo and Papara are slowly being absorbed into the urban center. Even the island of Moorea has become almost a suburb of Papeete, now that there are regular air and sea links between the two neighbors.

With its modern harbor facilities and Faaa Airport, Papeete is now a major stop for shipping and flights across the Pacific. French Polynesia's exports are transported from Papeete port, and a power plant supplies electricity for the island.

The town center faces the harbor. Most buildings are modern and two to three stories high. Government buildings and the courts of justice are located in the administrative sector, which starts at the foot of the hill. In contrast to the rest of the town, Vaiami Hospital and the naval regiment are still housed in beautiful colonial buildings. Around the administrative sector is the commercial section of town, with banks and offices. To the north lies Fare Ute industrial zone, with warehouses and branch offices of companies located in the town center. The missionary quarter is south of the town center. Catholic and Protestant schools stand next to small residential houses.

The residents of Papeete enjoy its greenery and warm weather, but luxury cars and fashionable restaurants are out of the reach of many.

The main street of Papeete is Boulevard Pomare, which curves around the harbor. It is lined by modern shopping malls, libraries, museums, and churches. The post office and the public swimming pool are also located there.

Beyond the town center is a motley collection of slums, middle-income houses, businesses, and industrial zones. Six of Tahiti's 21 communes (administrative districts) are in Papeete: Paea, Punaauia, Faaa, Pirae, Arue, and Mahina. The lower income groups can be found in Faaa, Paea, and the western side of Mahina. The higher grounds of Pirae and Punaauia are reserved for the beautiful houses of more affluent residents.

Papeete is home to 70,000 inhabitants, about one-third of the total population of French Polynesia. The population is still growing as more islanders leave their native villages to look for work in the capital.

CLIMATE

As Tahiti lies in the tropics, the climate is warm almost year-round. There are roughly two seasons: hot and rainy from November to April, with average temperatures ranging from 72°F to 90°F (22–32°C), and relatively cool and dry from May to October, with temperatures between 64°F and 72°F (18–22°C). The temperature decreases with altitude; in the cool season, nighttime temperatures on Mount Orohena can even drop to the freezing point.

The climate of Tahiti is tempered by cooling breezes from the sea. In the hot season, the prevailing winds are the northeast trade winds. In the cool season, it is the strong southeast trade wind, called *maraamu* ("mah-rah-AH-moo"), that dominates. A mountain wind called *hupe* ("HOO-pay") blows down onto the plain in the evening.

Rainfall is erratic, with Papeete recording an average of 73 inches (185 cm) yearly. The northeast trade winds bring the most rain, and Papenoo, in the northeast, receives twice as much rain as Punaauia on the western coast. Devastating floods are frequent in the Papenoo Valley during the rainy season. The mountainous region in the center of the island also receives much rain. Most rain falls from December to March. Humidity is high throughout the year, reaching 98% during the hotter months. Tahiti can also be hit by cyclones, which occur from January to March. Cyclone Veena in 1983 registered winds of up to 140 miles (225 km) per hour and is still remembered by Tahitians for the damage it caused.

Storm clouds build over Rangiroa, an atoll in French Polynesia. The region experiences heavy rain and thunderstorms from December to March.

FLORA

Tahiti used to be covered with forests of hibiscus, casuarina, rosewood, and chestnut. Along the coast, only a few pockets subsist today. However, hibiscus is quite common on higher ground.

The plant life of Tahiti varies according to the altitude. Along the coast, aside from the pockets of forest, a variety of tropical trees grow in profusion, including coconut palms, pandanus, and almond trees. The hillsides and valleys support fruit trees like guava, mango, lime, grapefruit, and orange. Other fruits that are planted on a large scale are pineapples, papaya, and bananas. Vanilla and coffee grow in the valleys and on the plateaus. Flowering trees include lantana, acacia, and ylang ylang. One interesting feature of Tahitian flora is that there are no plants with thorns, so Tahitians can walk barefoot without getting injured.

The sweet-smelling *tiare* is Tahiti's national flower. A festival is held in its honor in December.

On the slopes from 1,500 to 2,700 feet (457 m to 823 m), the vegetation consists mainly of a few trees and ferns that grow in dense clumps. Farther up, forests of hardwood trees start again. This is called the "forest of clouds," and because of the high humidity tree trunks are covered with epiphytes and other creepers. The strong winds blow the trunks into strange, tortuous shapes.

Tahiti's national flower is the *tiare Tahiti*, from the gardenia family. The small, white, sweet-smelling flowers are used to make headdresses and garlands or simply worn behind the ear. Tahitians have a long-standing love affair with flowers. Roads are lined with hibiscus, frangipani, bougainvillea, and flame of the forest, and even the humblest house is decorated with bright flowers.

FAUNA

Land fauna in Tahiti is rather scarce. Many of the animals on the island were introduced by the first Polynesians to come to the islands. The wild pig, with a mane at the neck, a long snout, tusks, and long legs, was the first animal to be brought into Tahiti. It is becoming rare due to hunting, so it is protected from extinction by a law regulating the number of pigs killed. Wild chickens exist in the coastal regions, and herds of wild goats roam the plateaus of Fautaua and Tuauru. The early Polynesians also brought dogs, and rats and lizards stowed away on the canoes. Europeans introduced domestic animals such as horses, cows, and cats.

Several types of fish are found in the rivers of Tahiti, including eels, jacks, eleotridae, kemeridae, gobies, mullets, and syngnathidae. The most

A noddy, one of the many species of birds in Tahiti. It lives on small fish and other marine life that it procures from the surface of the open seas beyond the reefs.

abundant are the eels, of which there are three species. Eared eels, however, have almost disappeared from Tahiti's rivers. In addition, there are four species of freshwater shrimp, a few mollusks, and some insects.

The waters off the coast of Tahiti are richer in animal life. Seven hundred species of fish inhabit the lagoon, and sharks and reptiles can be found beyond the reef. Tropical fish are colorful, and some, like the grouper, can grow to substantial dimensions. The green turtle and hawksbill turtle are quite common. Sea-snakes can also be found in the water, but they are very rare.

There are about 90 species of birds in Tahiti, most of them indigenous to French Polynesia. One of the most impressive is the tropic-bird, with its two long, red tail feathers. These feathers were prized as royal emblems in ancient Tahiti. Of the land birds, the Tahitian swallow is one of the most common.

None of the many insects in Tahiti is harmful to people, except for the mosquito, which carries diseases such as filariosis and dengue fever. The *tupa* is a land crab that digs holes and tunnels near the lagoon. There are also a number of snails, and the tiny *Partula* is used for making necklaces.

Turtles thrive in Polynesia's warm, tropical waters.

HISTORY

FOR A LONG TIME the people of Tahiti led a serene life away from, and unknown to, the rest of the world. They had no writing system and did not work with metal—in fact, they did not work at all, as the Europeans knew work. Apart from a few hours of fishing or collecting food, they spent most of the day enjoying themselves.

However, almost right from the moment the island was discovered by European explorers, it started to attract visitors lured by the myths of the "noble savage" and of an idyllic paradise on earth. Colonization and "civilization" brought diseases and evils that did not exist previously. The lifestyle on Tahiti was irremediably changed.

Tahiti was always described by those who visited the island in terms of what they felt or perceived, never for what it was. Even today, its rich pre-discovery history is overshadowed by the events related by the first European explorers. Perceptions remain of a gentle people leading an idyllic lifestyle. The reality is of a subjugated people who are now demanding their freedom back. The Tahitians, who warmly welcomed the colonizers, want to have more say in their country's destiny.

"This is the first time my reading has tempted me to visit a country other than my own."

—Denis Diderot, French philosopher, about Tahiti

Opposite: **The tomb of Pomare V, the last king of Tahiti.**

A POLYNESIAN "NOBLE SAVAGE"

On Captain James Cook's second voyage to Tahiti, a young man named Omai, from the island of Raiatea, boarded Cook's ship and sailed to England with the English expedition. Omai acted as translator on the other islands they visited and was greeted with much interest on his arrival in England. European romantic literature of the 18th century glorified the idealized concept of the "noble savage," who symbolized goodness untouched by civilization. Omai, who seemed to be the typical "noble savage," was presented to the king and introduced to famous people. He attended balls and parties, and even inspired a few successful plays. Omai returned to Tahiti with Cook in 1777, but felt alienated from his own people.

The Polynesians carved *tiki* ("tee-KEE"), statues that depicted gods, spirits, and ancestors. This ancient tiki is preserved at the Gauguin Museum.

POLYNESIAN ANCESTORS

The first people to settle in Polynesia came from Southeast Asia. Traveling east, they settled in Fiji around 1500 B.C., then Tonga and Samoa a few centuries later. From these islands, they set sail for what is now French Polynesia in around A.D. 300, settling first in the Marquesas. Over the next 1,000 years, they settled Easter Island, Hawaii, the Society Islands, and New Zealand.

Overpopulation on one island led the Polynesians to set off in search of new islands. At first, a voyage was made to explore for suitable islands. Once a sufficiently large island was found, the explorers noted its direction in relation to the stars and returned home to fetch their families, animals, and plants so as to establish settlements.

The ancient Polynesians were great navigators. They traveled in large double-hulled canoes, using the movements of the sun and the stars to direct them. They were also able to guess that land was near by noting changes in waves.

In 1976, the *Hokulea*, an oceangoing canoe built from ancient designs, sailed from Hawaii to Tahiti using only traditional navigational techniques based on the stars and the swells of waves. This voyage proved beyond doubt that the ancient Polynesians were the greatest sailors of all time.

By sailing a raft called *Kon-Tiki* from Peru to islands east of Tahiti in 1947, Swedish explorer Thor Heyerdahl tried to prove that the Polynesians actually came from South America. However, this theory has been largely debunked because corn—the staple food in South America—does not exist in Polynesia. If the Peruvians had colonized the islands, they would certainly have brought their staple food along.

TAHITI BEFORE THE EUROPEANS

Ancient Tahitian society was highly hierarchical. There were three distinct classes: *arii* ("ah-REE-ee," high chiefs), *raatira* ("rah-AH-tee-rah," minor chiefs and landowners), and *manahune* ("mah-nah-HOO-nay," common people). People from the different classes did not mix with each other, and children born of the union of a chief and a commoner were killed. Men and women were segregated most of the time, especially at meal times, and women could not participate in religious ceremonies.

The *arii* had absolute authority over his subjects, who considered him almost a god. He had to be physically higher than everyone else and was carried everywhere by his subjects. When he was standing, the subjects had to sit down; when he was seated, they had to lie down.

The *manahune* were servants, farmers, and fishers. They could not move out of their class unless they became priests or warriors. In between the chiefs and the commoners were the landowners. The landowners owed the same respect to the chiefs as the *manahune*, and their authority was limited to transmitting orders from the chiefs to the commoners and seeing that they were carried out.

Tahiti was divided into several districts, each ruled by an *arii*. Wars frequently broke out between the different tribes, and the vanquished were taken as slaves by the victors.

Although the ancient Polynesian society is gone forever, modern Tahitians perform historical reenactments as part of their festivals.

EUROPEAN DISCOVERY

On June 17, 1767, Captain Samuel Wallis chanced upon the island of Tahiti during an exploratory trip in search of the southern land mass that was thought to balance the northern hemisphere. He anchored his ship, the *HMS Dolphin,* at Taiarapu in the southern part of the island. The next day, he sailed farther north looking for a more pleasant anchorage, and landed in Matavai Bay. Hundreds of canoes surrounded the ship, and the islanders seemed friendly at first. However, they then started pelting the crew with stones, and the Englishmen opened fire with their cannons. On June 24, Wallis took formal possession of the island for the British crown and called it King George III's Island. After a few more rounds of cannon firing, the Tahitians decided to cooperate with the invaders and supplied them with fresh water and food. The *Dolphin* left Tahiti after a few weeks, but news of the discovery did not reach England until a year later.

LOVE FOR A NAIL

The crew of the *Dolphin* found out that Tahitians were more attracted to nails than the usual offerings of beads, knives, and mirrors. The Tahitians would give enormous quantities of fruits, pigs, and chickens in return for a nail. The reason was simple: metal nails could be easily bent into fishhooks, which had previously been carved with much effort from mother-of-pearl.

In return for sexual favors, Tahitian girls asked the sailors for nails. As more and more of the *Dolphin's* crew went ashore to meet girls, the ship's master grew worried about where all the nails were coming from. The carpenter assured him that the ship's stock of nails was under lock and key. However, when they proceeded to check the ship they found that nails had been pulled out of the woodwork. And they soon discovered that two-thirds of the crew were sleeping on the deck because the nails their hammocks were slung on were gone. The ship's officers had to take swift action before the whole ship fell to pieces. One man was punished as a scapegoat, and the crew was warned that they would face dire punishment if anyone was caught going ashore with a nail.

Two French ships, the *Etoile* and *Boudeuse* under the command of Louis-Antoine de Bougainville, arrived in Tahiti in April 1768. Unaware of the visit of Wallis and the English claim to the island, Bougainville claimed Tahiti for France, giving it the name of New Cythera, in reference to the birthplace of the Greek goddess of love, Aphrodite. Back in France, he promoted the idea of an idyllic land where a gentle people lived on the bounty of the land and sea, free from the restrictions of European life. Bougainville's recollections of Tahiti were published in 1771 in a book entitled *Voyage autour du monde*. The book was a resounding success and started the myth of the island paradise.

The third European associated with Tahiti was the English explorer Captain James Cook, who visited the island four times between 1769 and 1777. During his first visit, he stayed three months to observe the transit of the planet Venus across the sun. He traveled around the whole island and drew a precise map of Tahiti. With him came two botanists, Joseph Banks and Daniel Solander, who collected an enormous number of new species of plants, birds, fish, and insects, which added greatly to the scientific knowledge of the time. Cook's subsequent voyages enabled him to give the world further details of Polynesian society.

At the time of Tahiti's discovery by Europeans, the population stood at around 150,000. The Europeans brought diseases that ravaged the delicate constitution of the Tahitians: syphilis, tuberculosis, smallpox, and dysentery. By 1865, only 7,169 inhabitants remained.

Captain James Cook was the greatest of the Pacific maritime explorers. He recorded the lifestyle and customs of the Tahitians and took a real interest in their culture. After his first visit to Tahiti, he sailed west and became the first European to chart the coasts of New Zealand and eastern Australia.

MUTINY ON THE BOUNTY

In 1788, Lieutenant William Bligh came to Tahiti on board the *HMS Bounty* to collect young breadfruit trees to take to the West Indies. Bligh and his crew lived among the Tahitians for five months, and it was with reluctance that the crew set sail for Jamaica. Partly due to Bligh's severe treatment of his crew, many men sided with Fletcher Christian when he decided to get rid of the ship's commander and return to blissful Tahiti. Bligh was abandoned on the open sea with 18 loyal men and some basic supplies. In one of the most impressive open boat journeys in history, Bligh sailed 3,600 miles (5,792 km) to the Dutch Indies (Indonesia), suffering only one casualty on the way.

The mutineers first tried to settle in the Austral Islands but had to withdraw to Tahiti in the face of the inhabitants' hostility. Sixteen of them decided to stay in Tahiti. Christian, the rest of the crew, and a group of Tahitians sailed the *Bounty* to the uninhabited island of Pitcairn, where they burned the ship and founded the island's first settlement. The men who settled in Tahiti were recaptured by a British ship less than two years later. Four drowned in a shipwreck on the return trip, and the survivors were court-martialed in England. Three men were hanged.

The *Bounty* drama inspired three movies, made in 1935, 1962, and the 1980s.

MISSIONARIES AND COLONIAL POLITICS

Thirty years after the island was discovered by Europeans, a shipload of missionaries from the London Missionary Society arrived in Tahiti to convert the "heathens" from their "idolatrous ways." It took them 15 years to make their first convert, King Pomare II, who realized that the missionaries could be very useful to his rule and that British commerce was important for the island. The Pomare clan had gained access to firearms through their association with the European explorers, enabling them to gain supremacy over the whole island and establish Pomare I as the first king of Tahiti in 1790. After the conversion of Pomare II in 1812, all the people followed suit, and the ancient Polynesian religion disappeared forever.

For nearly 40 years, the Protestant missionaries enjoyed tremendous success in Tahiti. When Catholic missionaries arrived in 1835 with the intention of opening their own mission (having failed in a brief attempt in 1774), the Protestants used their influence over the reigning monarch, Queen Pomare IV, to send them away.

In 1837, George Pritchard, a Protestant missionary, became the English consul. He encouraged Queen Pomare to ask the British to make Tahiti a protectorate of the English crown. In 1842, French Admiral Abel Dupetit-Thouars arrived in Tahiti during the absence of both the English consul and the queen. With the help of the French consul, he organized the pro-French district chiefs to sign a demand for French protection. The French began to install themselves very firmly on the island, and after a series of threats, Queen Pomare was forced to ratify the demand for a protectorate. On September 9, 1842, Tahiti was proclaimed a French protectorate. A government was established that consisted of the royal commissioner, a military governor, and the captain of the port of Papeete.

King Pomare II was the first Tahitian to convert to Christianity. His son became Pomare III at the age of 1 year, but died six years later. Pomare II's daughter, Aimata, then became Pomare IV at the age of 14.

An old Catholic church in Moorea. Roman Catholic missionaries had little success in Tahiti until the region became a French protectorate.

THE FRENCH–TAHITIAN WAR

Queen Pomare was not happy with the fact that her personal flag was replaced by the official protectorate flag atop her palace. She protested to the king of France and looked to Britain for protection by taking refuge on the *HMS Basilisk*, an English ship anchored in Papeete harbor. This was the signal the population was waiting for; they immediately started a rebellion against the French invaders.

The first skirmishes took place in Taravao in March 1844. The following month, Governor Armand-Joseph Bruat engaged 400 men to carry out a bloody battle on Mahaena beach. The Tahitians lost 102 men and retreated to the Punaruu and Papenoo valleys to carry out guerrilla attacks on the French forces. The fighting spread to the other islands, and the Polynesians experienced some success in January 1846 in Huahine, prompting them to attack Papeete, where they were defeated. The French–Tahitian War lasted nearly three years, ending when the French troops launched a decisive attack on Fautaua fort in December 1846. Queen Pomare agreed to accept the protectorate over Tahiti and Moorea on January 7, 1847.

ÉTABLISSEMENTS FRANÇAIS DE L'OCÉANIE

At the time of the protectorate, the central structure of Tahitian administration was composed of the royal court, the Assembly, and the district councils. French authority was represented by the governor, assisted by various officers and civil servants. In 1866, the Tahitian legislative assembly voted for the introduction of French legislation, as proposed by the governor. When Pomare V abdicated in June 1880, all his territories were given to France in return for a pension of 5,000 francs a month, and Tahiti became a full-fledged French colony. In 1885, Tahiti and the other islands in the archipelago became the Établissements Français de l'Océanie (French Oceania).

This period was marked by the arrival of French and other colonizers. The French settlers were mainly soldiers and sailors who decided to stay on after demobilization. Having no income of their own, they tried their hand at agriculture, cultivating the lands of their Tahitian wives without much success. The English, Americans, and Germans were more successful because they came from a wealthier background. Those who married into the local aristocracy gained access to much land and capital. Thus were started the wealthy families that still rule the world of commerce in Tahiti: the Salmons, Laharragues, Branders, and Horts.

The Chinese were brought in as coolies to work in the cotton fields at Atimaono in the mid-1800s. Other immigrants came from Melanesia, the Gilbert Islands (now called Kiribati), Atiu, and Easter Island.

Many of the early Chinese immigrants returned to China when the cotton industry failed. Those who stayed went into business, setting up small grocery stores in the rural areas. This Chinese-owned store is on the island of Bora Bora.

27

INTERNAL AUTONOMY

Neglected by France, life in Tahiti was harsh at the beginning of the 20th century. Diseases and cyclones caused great destruction. However, with the opening of the Panama Canal in 1914, Tahiti became a port of call between Australia and the United States, and subsidies from the Colonial Office started to pour in. When World War I broke out, Tahiti sent a small contingent of volunteers for France.

After World War II, during which the Tahitian battalion earned honors at Bir Hakeim in North Africa, universal suffrage was granted to the Établissements Français de l'Océanie in 1945, and all residents of the colony were granted French citizenship. In 1947 a World War I volunteer, Pouvanaa a Oopa, created the "Pouvanaa Committee" to oppose the

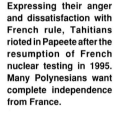

Expressing their anger and dissatisfaction with French rule, Tahitians rioted in Papeete after the resumption of French nuclear testing in 1995. Many Polynesians want complete independence from France.

A HISTORICAL CHRONOLOGY

600	First settlement of Tahiti
1767	Discovery of Tahiti by Samuel Wallis, who claims the island for the British crown
1768	Bougainville visits Tahiti and claims the island for France, calling it New Cythera
1769	Captain Cook spends three months at Matavai
1774	Spain sends missionaries, but they leave Tahiti after only a year
1788	William Bligh of the *HMS Bounty* arrives in Tahiti
1790	Pomare I conquers all of Tahiti and becomes the first king
1797	British Protestant missionaries arrive and settle at Matavai
1812	Pomare II renounces the ancient Polynesian religion and converts to Christianity
1827	Pomare III dies suddenly. His sister becomes Queen Pomare IV and rules for 50 years
1836	French Catholic missionaries expelled from Tahiti
1842	French protectorate proclaimed over Tahiti and Moorea
1844–46	The French–Tahitian War
1880	The protectorate is transformed into a French colony
1914	Papeete shelled by two German cruisers on September 22
1941–45	300 Tahitian volunteers fight in World War II
1957	Tahiti becomes a territory
1963	Construction of CEP; nuclear testing program initiated
1968	First hydrogen bomb exploded in Moruroa
1977	The local government is given wider powers
1984	Tahiti is granted full internal autonomy

arrival of further civil servants from France. From then on, there were more demands for autonomy in Tahiti. Thus, on July 27, 1957, the Établissements Français de l'Océanie changed from a colony to a territory and became known as French Polynesia. After General Charles de Gaulle came back to power in France in 1958, a referendum was held to allow Tahitians to decide whether they wanted to remain French or not. Nearly two-thirds of the electorate were in favor of the French commonwealth.

However, more and more voices were making themselves heard for greater autonomy. In 1977, Tahiti was granted a new statute giving the island slightly more say in its management. But it was not until 1984 that full internal autonomy came into effect. In the meantime, France had set up the Centre d'Expérimentation du Pacifique (CEP) on Moruroa island, and this was to have wide-ranging repercussions on Tahitian society.

GOVERNMENT

TAHITI AND THE REST of French Polynesia are part of the French DOM-TOM (Départements et Territoires d'Outre-Mer), which also includes Martinique and Guadeloupe in the Caribbean, Reunion in the Indian Ocean, and New Caledonia in the Pacific. Tahiti is an autonomous territory, which means that the island enjoys self-government as one district of French Polynesia.

However, the constitution of the Republic of France still remains the supreme law of the land, and Tahitians do not have much control over several aspects of their government. Pro-independence movements have made appeals to the United Nations Special Committee of 24, which helps colonies achieve independence, to put the territory on the priority list of states awaiting decolonization.

Opposite: **An antinuclear protest in Tahiti. The issue of nuclear testing has been closely linked to Tahitian demands for independence.**

THE TAHITIAN FLAG

The Tahitian flag, composed of one horizontal white stripe between two red stripes, disappeared after the death of Pomare V, the last king of Tahiti. It was reinstated in 1975 alongside the French national flag. In 1984, when the territory attained internal autonomy, the French government recognized the Tahitians' right to determine the symbols expressing the personality of their nation, and this was how the present flag came about. A stylized canoe in red floating above a blue sea with yellow rays of sun at the back was added to the middle of the previous flag. Today this flag represents the whole of French Polynesia and is flown side by side with the French tricolor.

THE TERRITORIAL ASSEMBLY

Tahiti, in common with the rest of French Polynesia, is governed by a territorial government made up of a president and eight to 10 ministers, who are in charge of public works, sports, health, social services, and primary education. The president is elected by the Territorial Assembly, which also ratifies the president's choice of ministers.

Legislative power is in the hands of the 41 members of the Territorial Assembly, who are elected for a period of five years. The territory is divided into districts, with 22 seats going to the district of Tahiti-Moorea, eight to the Leeward Islands, five to the Tuamotu and Gambier Islands, three to the Austral Islands, and three to the Marquesas. Because of the electoral system, one vote in the Tuamotus has the weight of three in Tahiti. The Assembly's primary function is to vote on the budget, but it can also dismiss the government through a motion of censure.

Outside of the two annual assembly sessions, a permanent commission is in place. In addition, the Economic and Social Committee brings together representatives from the various professions and establishes yearly reports.

French overseas departments and territories refer to France, particularly Paris, as the "Metropole."

FRANCE AND TAHITI

France is represented in the territory by a high commissioner. Assisted by a secretary-general, the high commissioner is in charge of the civil service, finance, national police, foreign affairs, immigration, defense, justice, communications, foreign trade, secondary and tertiary education, and the municipal councils. Despite the changes made by the new statute of 1984, the high commissioner still wields considerable power and can dissolve the Territorial Assembly or refer its decisions to an administrative tribunal.

French Polynesia is represented in Paris by two elected deputies in the National Assembly, as well as a senator and a social and economic councilor.

VOTING

As Tahitians are granted full French citizenship, all persons 18 and above are allowed to take part in national as well as local elections. Tahitians vote for members of the Territorial Assembly and for their representatives in the French National Assembly and Senate. They also participate in elections for the European Parliament. French civil servants and soldiers can vote in local elections (for the municipal councils and Territorial Assembly) the day they arrive in the territory, and the pro-French leading party in the Territorial Assembly is propped up mainly by votes from French expatriates working in Tahiti.

All men between the ages of 18 and 35—in Tahiti as in France—must serve one year of active duty in the army, navy, or air force. Those who are not fit for military service must serve two years of public service work or are deployed in other sectors of the government. Many of the French civil servants in Tahiti are actually young Frenchmen on military service.

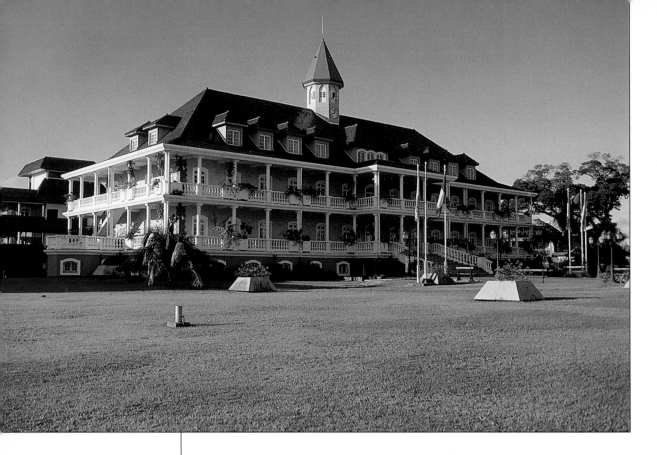

Papeete's town hall.

LOCAL GOVERNMENT

French Polynesia is divided into 48 communes, with 21 in Tahiti. The communes in the peninsula and the eastern half of Tahiti Nui are gathered into four groups of "associated communes." Each commune is managed by an elected municipal council, which chooses a mayor from its ranks. There are more than 900 municipal councilors throughout French Polynesia, elected by majority vote for a period of six years. Each commune elects a number of councilors based on its population size.

Each archipelago is run by an administrator appointed by the state, usually a French civil servant. He or she has almost complete control over the elected municipal councils. The administrators of the Windward, Tuamotu-Gambier, and Austral Islands are based in Papeete.

Local government is responsible for public hygiene, social services, and energy. Since French Polynesia achieved internal autonomy, it has also been responsible for the local police. One of the duties of the mayor is to solemnize marriages.

NATIONALISM

The first seeds of nationalism were sown by Pouvanaa a Oopa, an outspoken World War I hero from Huahine. In 1947, he founded the "Pouvanaa Committee," which became the Rassemblement Démocratique des Populations Tahitiennes (Tahitian Democratic Group, RDPT) in 1949. The RDPT was opposed to further deployment of French civil servants in Tahiti and wanted the country to move gradually toward independence. Pouvanaa's election to the French Chamber of Deputies in 1949 and to the vice-presidency of the Government Council in 1957 gave him immense opportunity to spread his separatist message among the population of Tahiti.

However, after he opposed General de Gaulle during the constitutional referendum of 1958, he was arrested on trumped-up charges of arson, sentenced to jail, and exiled from Tahiti. Pouvanaa was not freed until 1968, well after the nuclear-testing facilities were established. In a powerful political comeback, he was elected to the French Senate in 1971 and remained a senator until his death in 1977. Tahitians refer to him as *metua* (father), and Pouvanaa is credited as being the father of Tahitian nationalism. His statue stands outside the Territorial Assembly.

Pouvanaa's legacy has been the creation of several pro-independence political parties. However, Tahitian politics is full of nuances. Most parties are nationalistic, but not all favor full independence. Those that actively call for immediate independence from France are the Polynesian Liberation Front, the Let the People Take the Power party, and the Free Tahitians' Party. Most politicians, however, favor a milder form of independence, where Tahiti can enjoy complete self-government without severing its ties with France.

Nationalism is strongest on the island of Tahiti and weakest in the Tuamotu Islands and the Marquesas, which are heavily dependent on French aid. Much of the rioting that took place in Papeete in September 1995 following France's resumption of nuclear testing in the Pacific was blamed on separatists trying to publicize their cause to the rest of the world. However, it is strategically important for France to maintain a colony in the Pacific region. France does not want to lose this foothold in the Asia-Pacific region while other countries still have their bases, so it is unwilling to grant independence to Tahiti or the rest of French Polynesia.

A mushroom cloud rises from Moruroa after a nuclear detonation.

"The French treated us like rubbish, like rats. Now, you see what happens."

—Roti Make, a Tahitian, on the antinuclear rioting in 1995

NUCLEAR TESTING IN THE PACIFIC

After Algeria became independent of France in 1962, France decided to move its nuclear-testing facilities from the Sahara to the Tuamotu Islands in French Polynesia. Despite vocal protests from the local population, the Centre d'Expérimentation du Pacifique (CEP) was set up in 1963 on the atolls of Moruroa and Fangataufa, about 750 miles (1,207 km) from Tahiti. French military personnel were stationed in large numbers in Tahiti, and the French military presence is still strongly felt in the country. The CEP headquarters are located at Pirae, just east of Papeete, with a major support base opposite the yacht club at Arue.

The first bomb was exploded at Moruroa on July 2, 1966. Initially, nuclear testing took place in the atmosphere, but in 1974, after 44 atmospheric explosions and following strong international protests, the CEP decided to switch to underground tests, which are still carried out today. So far, more than 190 nuclear devices have been exploded.

In 1995, newly-elected French president Jacques Chirac unleashed a storm of protests worldwide when the French government announced that it would resume nuclear testing in French Polynesia after unofficially discontinuing testing for three years. Rioting broke out in Papeete, the passenger terminal at Faaa Airport was set on fire, and troops were called in from other territories to quell the unrest. Among the demonstrators were young unemployed Tahitians, supporters of Tahiti's independence, and antinuclear activists from various Pacific Rim countries. In the face of such strong sentiment, the French government reduced the number of devices exploded from eight to six and announced that those were the last tests.

IF IF IS SAFE
- Dump it in Tokyo
- Test it in Paris
- Store it in Wash-
  ington
But Keep My Pacific
Nuclear Free

WE DON'T WANT TO SUFFER!!

From the French point of view, nuclear testing is necessary in order to maintain France's position as a world political and military power. They dismiss the fears of Pacific Rim nations, arguing that nuclear test sites in Russia are actually closer to Paris that Moruroa is to its nearest neighbor.

France has always claimed that its underground tests were safe and that there was no possibility of radioactive leaks into the sea. However, in December 1990, a radiation expert from Greenpeace, an international environmental organization, collected some samples of the water around Moruroa and detected a high concentration of cobalt 60 and cesium 134, proving that the sea was already contaminated by radioactivity. In addition, various experts have pointed out the high number of cases of cancer and deformities in newborn babies in French Polynesia. Tahiti's political leaders are now demanding that the World Health Organization intervene to properly investigate radiation leaking from Moruroa. The latest series of nuclear tests in the Pacific has aroused world opinion against such destructive activity, but wildlife and nature in the waters off Moruroa are already irremediably damaged.

Protests against French nuclear testing in the Pacific have gone beyond the borders of French Polynesia. These children in Rarotonga are among the many Polynesians who believe that if the French must test nuclear weapons, they should do so in their own country.

ECONOMY

WITH THE SETTING UP of the Centre d'Expérimentation du Pacifique (CEP) in the 1960s, Tahiti was suddenly thrust into the modern world of consumerism. Instead of cultivating their own crops and fishing for their food, Tahitians became wage earners and had to depend on others to supply their food needs. Thousands are now employed by the CEP and other government bodies. Subsistence agriculture is mainly practiced in the smaller islands, while most residents of Tahiti lead an urban lifestyle, spending their free time shopping, watching movies, and having fun.

Above: **Papeete port is the hub of the region's trade.**

Opposite: **A woman sells colorful *pareus*, cloths that are the traditional Tahitian dress. Small craft industries cater to both the local and tourist markets.**

Inevitably, with economic activity becoming more sophisticated, unemployment keeps on rising. After the completion of the CEP and Faaa Airport, thousands of visiting workers from the rest of French Polynesia found themselves stranded in Tahiti, jobless. Today they are joined by more immigrants from the outer islands as well as young Tahitians leaving school with few qualifications. These jobless or occasional workers account for the growing slums on the outskirts of Papeete.

THE FRENCH PACIFIC FRANC

Unlike the French overseas departments, Tahiti does not use the French franc (FF) as legal tender. The currency in use in the whole of French Polynesia as well as New Caledonia is the French Pacific franc or *Cour de Franc Pacifique* (CFP). The relationship between the two currencies is fixed at 1 FF to 18.18 CFP.

French Pacific franc bills carry pictures of sailboats, flowers, coconut trees, and Polynesian people.

GOVERNMENT SPENDING

Tahiti is totally dependent on French government spending. Although the French government contributes very little to the territorial budget, it finances the numerous departments and services under the direct control of the high commissioner. The French government spends US$55 million a month in the territory, with two-thirds going to the military. Much of the rest is used to pay the salaries of the 2,000 expatriate government employees. Only one-third of all Tahitians get any direct benefit from French spending.

Residents of Tahiti, including French expatriates, do not pay personal income tax. However, the low-income group is hard hit by high indirect taxes, such as customs duties and value-added taxes. With the presence of the highly-paid and free-spending French civil servants, the cost of living in Tahiti is very high, and even with the help of unemployment and social security benefits, many Tahitians find it hard to make ends meet.

AGRICULTURE

Since much of Tahiti's interior is mountainous, very little land is devoted to agriculture. Agricultural activity takes place in four main areas: Papara commune, Teva I Uta commune, the isthmus and plateau of Taravao, and the east coast. However, agriculture is practiced on an intensive basis, making use of modern technology.

Nearly half of the lowlands of Papara are under cultivation. The commune produces vegetables, flowers, pork, and poultry. The neighboring commune of Teva I Uta specializes in vegetable production and cattle rearing. Cattle are raised on coconut plantations, and the coconut plantations of Teva I Uta are the largest in Tahiti. However, many of the coconut trees are more than 100 years old, and Tahiti accounts for only a small percentage of the copra production of the territory. Most of the commune's agricultural activity is concentrated in the coastal areas of Mataiea and Papeari. Dairy cattle are reared in Taravao, and citrus fruits—oranges in particular—and honey are also produced. The east coast of Tahiti is mostly devoted to subsistence farming, but flowers (anthuriums, *opuhi*, and orchids) are grown on a large scale in the districts of Mahaena and Tiarei.

Despite the use of modern farming methods and machinery, agricultural production does not satisfy local demand. Many products are imported from other islands or other countries, New Zealand in particular. To make the situation worse, much of the land under cultivation is being taken over by residential development, especially in Papara, Mahaena, and Tiarei.

French Polynesia is a major producer of vanilla. This variety is native to the Pacific region and is called *Vanilla tahitensis*, or Tahiti vanilla.

TRADE

Tahiti suffers from a severe imbalance in trade, with imports amounting to nearly 10 times its exports. Much of this imbalance is consumed by the French administration, and 28% of imports are related to nuclear testing. Half of all imports come from France, which has imposed a series of self-favoring restrictions. Imports include food, fuel, building materials, consumer goods, and automobiles. The main exports are copra (the dried white flesh of the coconut), which is crushed into coconut oil and animal feed in a mill in Papeete, and cultured pearls. Copra and pearls are not produced on the island of Tahiti itself but in the Tuamotus and other outer islands. Tahiti's main trading partners, apart from France, are Japan, New Zealand, and other islands in the Pacific.

TOURISM

Tourism started in earnest with the opening of Faaa Airport in 1961. Today it is the main revenue sector of French Polynesia's economy. The tourist industry provides 4,000 jobs, and earnings from tourism cover 18% of the territory's import bill.

One-third of all tourists come from the United States. U.S., Australian, and Asian tourists regard Tahiti as a stopover destination, spending a couple of days in Papeete on their way to and from the United States. Tourists from France and other European countries stay longer, but not

Laying out coconuts to dry. The white flesh of the coconut is one of French Polynesia's major export products.

always in hotels. Most of them come to visit relatives or friends who are expatriate workers in Tahiti.

Tourism in French Polynesia is much less developed than in Hawaii. In Tahiti there is only one tourist for 100 residents, while Hawaii has 11. High prices and the distance from the United States, Europe, and Asia have kept tourist arrivals low. The most popular islands are Tahiti, Moorea, Huahine, Raiatea, and Bora Bora.

Tourists enjoy a boat ride through the clear blue waters near Tahiti.

FISHING

Fishing is practiced on an industrial scale by Japanese, Korean, and U.S. purse seiners and longline vessels that pay a total fee of about one billion French Pacific francs every year to the Tahitian government to fish in French Polynesia's territorial waters. Not more than 198 ships are allowed every year, and the amount of fish they can catch is limited to 11,900 tons. The catch is made up of deep-sea fish, mainly tuna, which is highly prized by the Japanese, as well as marlin and shark. Such intensive fishing requires heavy investment, and the locals do not have the means to practice it.

Tahitians fishing in the open sea do so in *bonitiers* ("boh-nee-TIAY"), 36-foot (11-m) boats propelled by a powerful motor. The bonitier can take two or three fishers out for one day to about 30 miles (48 km) from shore. Fishing is done with lines, and the shoals of fish are detected by the presence of birds hovering above the sea. In addition, several sunken barges placed near the coast attract big fish and make it easier to locate large concentrations of fish.

Lagoon fishing is much more common throughout the islands. It is practiced in small wooden boats powered by outboard motors. Swift and light, they are ideal for catching flying fish or *mahi mahi* (dorado or dolphinfish), which are harpooned as they swim by. Lagoon fishers are not professionals; most of them fish for their family meal. When they catch more fish than required, they keep it for the next day's meal.

Fishing is practiced on a small scale by ordinary Tahitians. It is common to see fish strung out by the side of the road.

BLACK PEARLS

The black pearl industry is the second largest source of revenue for French Polynesia, after tourism. Black pearls are raised in more than 65 cooperatives and farms in the Tuamotu and Gambier Islands where the *Pinctada margaritifera* (mother-of-pearl) oyster abounds.

To produce a pearl, an implant (a tiny spherical object) is introduced into the oyster, which coats it with mother-of-pearl secretion. This natural process takes two years. Implantation is performed almost exclusively by Japanese specialists, although more Tahitians are becoming proficient at it. After implantation, the oysters are returned to the sea tied to long ropes. As many as 20,000 oysters are raised at one time. But the success rate is very low: only 30 to 50% of the oysters actually produce a pearl.

Several types of pearl are harvested. "Keshis" are deformed pearls composed exclusively of mother-of-pearl. This occurs when the implant is rejected by the oyster after it has been returned to the sea. "Baroque" pearls have imperfections in shape. Perfect pearls are smooth and round, with a metallic green-gray or blue-gray color. Only 3% of the harvest is perfect.

The cooperatives sell their pearls at an auction in Papeete every October. Local jewelers vie with Japanese buyers at these events, with more than 40,000 black pearls changing hands. Private farms sell their production through independent dealers or plush retail outlets in Papeete.

LAW OF THE SEA

When President Harry Truman declared U.S. sovereignty over the natural resources of the adjacent continental shelf in 1945, other countries followed suit, and the United Nations convened a Conference on the Law of the Sea in 1958 that accepted national control over shelves up to 600 feet (183 m) deep. However, national claims multiplied so much that a second conference was convened, leading to the signing of the Law of the Sea convention in Jamaica in 1982.

The Law of the Sea states that a country can claim 12 nautical miles of sea off its shores as its territorial waters. (One international nautical mile is equal to around 1.15 miles, or 1.85 km.) A country's continental shelf extends 200 nautical miles offshore. This area is called the Exclusive Economic Zone (EEZ), and the state has full control over all resources, living and non-living, contained in the zone.

French Polynesia can lay claim to over three million square miles (7.8 million square km) of the continental shelf, with immense possibilities for development. The National Marine Research Center estimates that vast mineral deposits, such as nickel, cobalt, manganese, and copper, are scattered across Tahiti's EEZ. While giving more political weight (and mineral wealth) to oceanic states, the Law of the Sea has also made French Polynesia much more valuable to France. The French government has adamantly refused to give the Territorial Assembly any jurisdiction over its EEZ, an indication that it does not plan to let go of its sovereignty over the islands.

LE TRUCK

Public transportation in Tahiti is provided by a network of privately-owned minibuses called *le truck* ("luh TRUCK"). The driver's cabin is separated from the passengers' section by a panel, and the passenger door is at the back. The destination is written on the front. Passengers sit on long wooden benches, and bags and other bulky items are piled on the roof of the truck. A notice advises passengers to hang their fish from the back of the truck. The vehicles are painted in bright colors, and the network covers the whole island. The central terminal is near Papeete market, and the last trucks leave for the outlying districts at about 5 p.m. Around town, the service does not stop until 10 or 11 p.m. On Sundays, however, no truck runs after 12 noon.

The starting point—usually Papeete—and the final destination are indicated at the front of the truck. Other district names along the route are painted on the sides. No truck goes round the whole island, and long journeys involve catching several *trucks*. In town and the districts of Pirae and Faaa, bus stops are designated by diagonal white lines painted on the street, sometimes with a sign. Elsewhere there is no specific bus stop; passengers just wave the trucks down wherever they happen to be. There is no fixed schedule, but trucks are more frequent in and around Papeete. Fares are quite cheap and are usually posted on the side of the truck.

Inside the trucks are mammoth speakers blasting rock music or reggae. At night they take on a different look. Many have softly-colored lights inside and play Tahitian ballads instead of the loud daytime music.

Above: **After they have alighted from the *truck*, passengers walk around to the side of the vehicle and pay the driver through the window.**

Opposite: **The Tahiti–Moorea ferry departing Moorea. Oceanic states like French Polynesia rely on boats and light aircraft for inter-island travel.**

47

TAHITIANS

ALL TAHITIANS are French citizens. Whatever their ethnic background, they enjoy the same constitutional rights as any citizen of France.

Slightly fewer than 200,000 people live in French Polynesia, with more than half living in Tahiti. Since large areas of Tahiti's land surface are not fit for human settlement, most people live in the coastal regions. About 70% of Tahitians live along the northwest coast, in and around Papeete, in the districts of Papeete, Pirae, Arue, and Mahina. This small area supports more than 1,500 persons per square mile (579 per sq. km).

Tahiti and the neighboring island of Raiatea are the only melting pots in the whole territory. The population on these islands is composed of Polynesians, Europeans (mainly French), Chinese, and people of mixed descent (Polynesian/European, Polynesian/Chinese or Chinese/European).

In Tahiti, about 60% of the population is Polynesian, 15% European, 15% mixed, and 10% Chinese. Nearly half of the population is under the age of 20. People over 60 account for only about 5% of the total population.

Above: **A young Tahitian couple holding a bunch of taro, a kind of root vegetable.**

Opposite: **Polynesians make up the largest portion of Tahiti's population.**

CHANGES IN TAHITI'S POPULATION

A graph of the population of Tahiti shows a sharp decline in the decades following the discovery of the island by the European explorers. However, since the beginning of this century, the Tahitian population has been slowly rebuilding itself through a higher survival rate at birth, longer life expectancy, and immigration. Life expectancy in Tahiti is 64 years, compared to 75 in France.

Although descended from a migrating people, Tahitians do not travel much beyond the territory. A small group of Tahitian mine workers live in New Caledonia. On the other hand, migrants from Australia and Europe are still coming to settle in Tahiti, although in smaller numbers than in the 1970s.

POLYNESIANS

The Polynesians were the first inhabitants of Tahiti. Their ancestors traveled by canoe from Southeast Asia to settle in the scattered islands of the Polynesian Triangle. They call themselves *Taata Maohi* ("tah-AH-tah mah-OH-hee") or *Taata Tahiti*, meaning "people of Polynesia."

Like many Tahitians, this child has acquired a taste for French bread.

The Polynesian people have the same coloring as their distant ancestors: straight black hair, black eyes, and burnished skin. They have wide-set eyes, a round nose, and full lips. A sporty people, they tend to be well-built and graceful. A sedentary modern lifestyle, however, is changing their physical profile, and obesity and its attendant health problems are becoming more pronounced.

Polynesians have always loved children, and attractive government child benefits do not encourage family planning. For these reasons, Polynesian families tend to be large, with as many as 10 children. In addition, adoption is a traditional feature of Polynesian society.

Like most other colonized peoples, the Taata Maohi have lost much of their land to the colonizers and are relegated to the bottom of the economic and social ladder. Most of them are farmers, fishers, or manual workers. The Polynesian culture teaches a sense of sharing and reciprocal generosity, and the pursuit of money and material wealth is alien. Unemployment is rife among Polynesians. Their economic and cultural situation has resulted in the growth of nationalism, and most Polynesians favor separatism from France.

A tusk necklace and a headdress of palm fronds adorn this Polynesian man.

MAUI, THE POLYNESIAN SUPERHERO

Maui was a demigod who reveled in playing tricks and upsetting the status quo. One of his most well-known exploits was slowing down the passage of the sun. Before this feat, the sun used to race across the sky, and days were not long enough for people to beat out and dry tree bark for making cloth, grow and prepare food, and build temples to the gods.

To slow down the sun, Maui braided several lassoes, which he threw round the rays of the sun. They all broke, except the one made from the hair of his sister Hina. From then on the sun was bound to a boulder on the beach and traveled at a more convenient pace. As proof of this exploit, Tahitians point to his footprints, which can still be seen on the reef at Vairao on the peninsula.

Other feats performed by this superhero are lifting the sky high enough to permit people to walk upright, stealing fire from the gods to give to humans (the Polynesian equivalent of the mythical Greek hero, Prometheus), and fishing up all the islands of Polynesia out of the sea with a magical hook made from the jawbone of his grandmother. Maui was the archetypal hero who could deal with both gods and humans.

DEMIS

The offspring of early marriages between Polynesians and European colonizers, *Demis* ("doh-MEE") are also called *Afa* ("AH-fah") *Tahiti*, meaning "half Polynesian." The Demis population displays the whole spectrum of skin color typical of their ancestors, with many looking no different from Polynesians.

A lavish *Demis* wedding.

Although there are also many poor farmers among the Demis, this group is, on the whole, wealthier than the Polynesians. Fluent in both French and Tahitian, the Demis population acts as a link between the French administration and the local people, although they identify more with European culture. Starting out as traders and landowners, Demis are now teachers, civil servants, and professionals. The largest business firms in the country are in the hands of a few Demis families. These wealthy Demis do not identify at all with the Polynesians, although they have Polynesian relatives.

Demis families own large tracts of land in Tahiti. When their European ancestors arrived in Tahiti, they married the daughters of the tribal chiefs. The land, which used to be owned collectively by the tribe, became the property of the chiefs at the time of colonization, and from them passed on to their mixed descendants. This was how the Salmon family, from whom came Queen Marau, the last queen of Tahiti, became one of the most prominent families in the country.

CHINESE

The first Chinese came to Tahiti during the American Civil War, when the supply of cotton to Europe was disrupted. In 1865–66, a British colonizer recruited 1,010 laborers from the southern Chinese province of Guangdong to work in the cotton fields of Atimaono because the local Polynesians could not be persuaded to do such heavy work. However, at the end of the war the cotton industry went bankrupt, and most of them returned to China.

About 300 Chinese stayed on in Tahiti, taking on gardening jobs or becoming shopkeepers. They were joined in 1910 by a later group of immigrants fleeing the poverty of their native land. Chinese immigration did not end until World War II. As the government did little to integrate the *Tinito* ("tee-NEE-toh," Chinese) community into Tahitian society, refusing to grant them the right to own land and closing the door to the professions, the Chinese immigrants turned their energy to the retail trade. In a few decades they were in control of the retail trade and of transactions involving vanilla and mother-of-pearl and were investing large capital in maritime transportation.

A Tahitian of Chinese descent.

In 1964 the French government decided to assimilate the Chinese community by granting them citizenship, requiring that they adopt French names and closing all Chinese schools. Despite becoming French citizens, the Chinese community is still distinct, keeping its language and ancestral customs alive through cultural associations and clan groups. The Chinese shopkeeper is a common sight in all the islands of French Polynesia, and entire streets are lined with Chinese stores in Papeete.

Local women greet a group of French sailors. French military personnel like these form a large proportion of *Popaa* in Tahiti and its neighboring islands.

POPAA

All white people are called *Popaa* ("poh-pah-AH"), meaning foreigner, by the Tahitians. The French are also called *Popaa Farani* ("poh-pah-AH fah-rah-NIH"). There is no traditional white community in Tahiti because the former colonizers married Polynesian women and their descendants are Demis rather than Popaa. Most Popaa are French soldiers and civil servants and are only temporary residents of Tahiti. About 20,000 live in French Polynesia, many employed by the CEP and supporting industries. There was also considerable European immigration in the 1960s and 1970s.

The profile of the Popaa population is peculiar in that 62% of Popaa are male, due to the heavy presence of the military in Tahiti. On the whole, the Popaa community is young and always changing.

Many Popaa come to Tahiti, live and work in the country, and leave without learning a single word of Tahitian or ever mixing with Polynesian society. Because of the high salary and other perks offered to French civil servants and administrators, a tour of duty in Tahiti is highly desirable and is treated like a long vacation. The Popaa can be expelled from Tahiti if their actions are harmful to the country. However, this does not usually happen.

TAHITIAN DRESS

The image that has gone round the world of the bare-breasted *vahine* ("vah-HEE-nay," woman) dressed in a grass skirt with a garland of flowers round her neck can only be found on tourist brochures. The traditional dress for both men and women is the *pareu* ("pah-RAY-oh"), a 6-ft (1.8-m) length of cotton cloth printed with bright designs, usually flowers. There are several ways for women to wear a pareu. The simplest is to wrap the cloth around the body and tuck the ends in. For a more secure fit, the pareu is wrapped around the body, one corner thrown over the right shoulder, the other corner passed under the left arm and the two ends tied at the neck. Men wear the pareu as a loin cloth, tied around the waist.

When the missionaries arrived in Tahiti, they were shocked by the state of undress of the women, in particular, and designed a "mission dress" for them. This is a loose cotton dress with wrist- or elbow-length sleeves, much like a nightgown. Cool and comfortable, it is still worn by Tahitian women and is the uniform of singing *himene* ("hee-MAY-nay") groups.

Most Tahitians, however, dress in stylish Western clothes. Young girls wear jeans and T-shirts or skirts and blouses. At the beach or for casual wear, shorts and cropped tops are common. Tahitian men wear shirts and trousers to work and shorts and T-shirts at home. Men and women put on shoes to go out, although they may walk barefoot in the house.

Himene singers wearing brightly-printed mission dresses and flower headdresses.

LIFESTYLE

MOST OF THE POPULATION of Tahiti is concentrated in and around Papeete. Residents work in the airport, at the docks, and in businesses in town. The rural Tahitians are farmers and fishers, mostly at subsistence level.

Great differences in income create several distinct social classes, and since the cost of living is very high, many Tahitians live on the brink of poverty. In addition, high unemployment among the young has resulted in severe social problems such as drug addiction, alcoholism, and crime.

However, in spite of difficult living conditions, the Tahitian people have not lost their ability to enjoy themselves. They take pleasure in simple activities, like listening to music or riding around the island on their scooters.

Left: **Tahitians have a strong sense of family and community, and they enjoy gatherings and communal activities.**

Opposite: **Making fish traps in the traditional way.**

CLASS STRUCTURE

The Tahitian social structure is very much related to ethnic backgrounds. The white Popaa are at the top of the social ladder, followed by the Demis and the Chinese, with the Polynesians at the bottom. Class stratification is based not so much on heritage as on income.

UPPER CLASS The upper class is formed by the French civil servants and administrators, who are paid salaries that are 84% higher than their counterparts in France. In addition to generous expatriation benefits, they do not have to pay income tax, since there is no personal income tax in French Polynesia. Most Popaa government officials serve a three-year term in the territory, at the end of which they are entitled to six months' paid leave. Although they try to get into the spirit of life in Polynesia, by wearing flowery shirts to work, for example, the ruling class lives apart from the local population. Their exalted status attracts much resentment from the local population, who would like to see fewer French officials and more of their own people in charge of their country.

MIDDLE CLASS   The middle class is made up of Demis, people of mixed ancestry. Although some Demis have much higher incomes through their businesses than Popaa, they are not considered to be on an equal footing with the French community. Many Demis families are wealthy landowners who derive their income from leasing the land to farmers or developing their property into commercial ventures. Since they have always had access to formal education, the Demis hold jobs in the government service and the professions and still keep a strong hold on the business sector. They are fluent in French and Tahitian, and many can also speak English. Culturally closer to their European roots, they are faced with a situation where the two sides of their ancestry are at odds with each other. Economically powerful, they are neither the rulers of their country nor do they have any political clout. However, most Demis are against independence and side with the French population in political matters.

This family is able to enjoy a large-screen television in their middle-class home.

In terms of income, the Chinese community also belongs to the middle class. Having succeeded in the retail trade, they have moved into bigger businesses and bought up large areas of property since they were granted French citizenship. Today, most Chinese manage their own businesses, and many young people, having received a formal French education, are professionals. However, they are not represented in the government. The Chinese have economic power, but they have no cultural ties with the traditional Demis middle class. Having long been viewed as an economic threat to the local wealthy class, this community is slowly integrating into Tahitian society through marriage with Polynesians and Popaa, forming a new, ethnically different Demis group. The Chinese community is politically fragmented, with one group favoring independence and the other preferring the status quo that has allowed them to amass their wealth.

LOWER CLASS   The majority Polynesian ethnic group forms the lower class. Despoiled of their land during colonization, the rural Polynesians subsist on farms rented from the wealthy landowners. Those who own land are vegetable farmers, supplementing their diet with fish that they catch themselves. Most other Polynesians are employed as manual workers, in the construction industry, or in tourism. Unemployment among Polynesians is very high. An estimated 20,000 poor, unemployed, and marginalized Polynesians live in slums on the outskirts of the capital. In the shanty towns behind Papeete and Faaa, 10 to 15 Polynesians live crammed into each neat flower-decked plywood house. Polynesian families tend to be larger than those of other ethnic groups. Disaffected Polynesian youths were responsible for much of the looting and violence committed during the antinuclear protests of September 1995. The poor urban communities view independence from France as their only means of salvation.

At the opposite end of the social scale from the Popaa are the poor rural class and the slum-dwellers of Papeete, most of whom are Polynesian.

A small group of poor Demis is also part of the lower class. Because of their poverty, they feel closer to the Polynesian section of the population. To all intents and purposes, these Demis are treated as Polynesians.

A modern version of the traditional Tahitian house, made of painted plywood and thatched with palm leaves.

THE TAHITIAN HOUSE

The traditional Tahitian residence consists of several separate buildings instead of rooms. The *fare tutu* ("fah-RAY too-TOO") is the kitchen, while the dining area is called *fare tamaa* ("fah-RAY tah-MAH-ah"). The sleeping quarters are located in another building called *fare taoto* ("fah-RAY tah-OH-toh"). In addition, toilet and bathing facilities are located in separate buildings. The traditional building materials are coconut trunks and pandanus leaves.

Today very few Tahitians live in the traditional house. Housing design has been replaced by Western architectural models. In the rural areas, houses are square, built of wood and covered with a sloping thatch roof. In the affluent suburbs of Papeete, people live in beautiful detached houses made of concrete and fronted by flower-filled gardens. Most working-class Tahitians, however, are housed in double-story row houses made of plywood. These are small, afford almost no privacy, and have no garden. Although such houses are ugly and uncomfortable, public housing is still better than the slums, where several families share a house, and as many as 20 people live in one room.

Tahua do not receive any monetary payment for their services. Instead, patients leave a gift of food on the floor. Neither party acknowledges the gift.

HEALTH CARE

Health care in Tahiti is of the same standard as that of France, with 40 doctors in Papeete's Mamao Hospital treating almost every type of disease and the military hospital of Jean Prince at Pirae specializing in the treatment of burns. The hospitals in the other towns all possess an operating room, but severe cases are sent to Papeete.

Tahitians have three health care options: traditional remedies, private doctors, and public health services. *Raau Tahiti* ("rah-AH-oo tah-hih-TIH," traditional medicine) is composed of herbal remedies prepared at home, which are quite effective in the treatment of pains and aches, coughs, and fever. Traditional remedies are still very popular for cultural reasons and also because they are cheap. The traditional medicine man is called a *tahua* ("tah-HOO-ah") and gives treatments for free. Most people do not actually consult the tahua because the recipes for common remedies are passed down in the family from one generation to the next.

Private medical facilities are good, but expensive. They include general practitioners, specialists, and dentists. Two modern clinics, Paofai and Cardella, in Papeete offer surgical and maternity facilities. They also employ a number of doctors who give consultations to the sick. Public health care is free and is given at dispensaries, polyclinics, and hospitals. Schoolchildren receive regular free health screenings.

RAAU TAHITI

Some traditional treatments do not involve the preparation of herbal remedies. When stung by a sea urchin, just urinate on the injury. If stung by the crown-of-thorns starfish, turn the animal over and apply it to the wound. The suckers on the stomach of the starfish suck out the spines and venom. The stings of the scorpion fish and stonefish are treated by bathing the wound with the water contained in small black sea cucumbers.

EDUCATION

Tahitian children follow the French system of education. Schooling is compulsory between the ages of 6 and 16. After secondary school, the better students study three more years for the baccalaureate exams. Those who pass receive free university education.

Tahitian children study a completely French curriculum, learning French language, literature, history, and geography, and very little about their own part of the world. The local government is only in charge of primary

Tahitian children study an all-French curriculum.

education, while secondary and tertiary education is the domain of the high commissioner. The failure rate is very high, ranging from 40% to 60%. The best students are given scholarships by the government to enable them to go on studying, while the rest drop out of school. Every year, 3,000 children between the ages of 13 and 16 drop out of school. Only around one-quarter of young people aged 20 have an educational certificate.

There are two types of schools: government schools, which are free, and fee-paying private schools, usually run by the churches. Most primary schools are public, but more than half of the young people of Papeete attend a private secondary school. Many of the private schools receive government funding. In exchange for this, they must follow exactly the same curriculum as government schools.

Tertiary education is provided by the Université Française du Pacifique, opened in 1987 in Papeete.

SOCIAL PROBLEMS

One of the main problems faced by Tahitian society today is unemployment. The unemployed are mainly women, young people, people with few skills, and Polynesians. More than half of the people looking for work are in the 18–24 age group. They are the product of an educational system that does not take into consideration the local needs. Those who do have a certificate are not qualified for the types of jobs that are available. In addition to the unemployed, there are also wage earners who are employed on a periodic basis. Frequently out of work, but not registered as unemployed, they account for as much as 30% of the labor force.

Unemployment is a major problem. Polynesians who come from other islands and are unable to find work may end up living on the street or in a slum.

Resulting directly from the problem of unemployment is that of delinquency. This problem mostly affects young Polynesians who have dropped out of school at 16—the age when compulsory education ends— and are waiting to enlist in the military. With a lot of time on their hands and little money, and tempted by Papeete's consumer society, they turn to petty crime such as theft, cheating, or burglary. Young delinquents from low-income families live outside social norms. They tend to live in groups and call themselves *hombos* ("HOM-boh"). The word derives from the Spanish *hombre* (man) and is used to describe "antiheroes" such as Mexican and U.S. outlaws and comic book characters.

Many sociologists see the rise in delinquency as having social and cultural, rather than economic, roots. These young Polynesians turn to petty crime because they are confused about their own cultural identity, living in a world with two totally different cultures—Polynesian and French.

"We debauch their morals and introduce among them wants and diseases which they never before knew, and which disturb the happy tranquillity which they enjoyed."

—*Captain James Cook*

ALCOHOLISM AND DRUG ABUSE

One of the scourges of Tahiti, alcoholism causes great destruction among Polynesians and lower-income groups. Drinking beer is almost a rite of passage for young boys, who see it as taking a step into the adult world. The usual age at which boys start drinking alcohol is around 14. Drinking is very common among the lower class, and alcoholism and its negative effects are seen as unavoidable. People are impressed by good drinkers, and drunkenness can even be a source of pride. Drunkenness also affects women and young girls. Domestic violence is the most frequent consequence of excessive consumption of alcohol. Another result is road accidents caused by drunkenness. Tahiti holds the world record for the number of road deaths per mile of road.

Drug addiction is not as prevalent as drunkenness, but is cause for concern since children as young as 10 years old have been caught abusing solvents. Hard drugs, such as heroin or cocaine, are still not very common in Tahiti, but the cultivation of marijuana is spreading in the humid, mountainous regions of the interior.

VAHINE

Two centuries ago, Bougainville wrote that Tahitian vahine were as pretty as European women and more well-proportioned. Since then, the myth of the gentle women of Tahiti, half-naked and beckoning to all new male arrivals, has taken root in Western imagination. The romanticized vahine has long black hair, a slim and supple body, and a bewitching smile.

Most Tahitian women are indeed pretty, graceful, and stylish. Women of all ages like to wear colorful hibiscus or frangipani blooms in their hair and wear bright, youthful colors. Even the poorest house dress is worn with style. Tahitian women wear very little jewelry, preferring the natural flowers that grow in profusion on their island. The art of making flower garlands and headdresses is passed down from mother to daughter. The flowers are picked before sunrise and it takes half an hour to make one simple headdress.

In the days when the first European explorers marveled at their apparent freedom, Tahitian women were in fact treated as second-class citizens. They were considered impure and were not allowed near sacred

THE THIRD SEX

Polynesia's *mahu* ("mah-HOO") bears little of the stigma attached to transvestites in the West. When the missionaries first arrived in Tahiti, they were shocked to discover that not only did the mahus exist, they were encouraged to do the jobs women normally do. They looked after children, worked as maids, and cooked, all the while wearing women's clothes or whatever they wanted to wear. In festivals and celebrations, they took the women's parts.

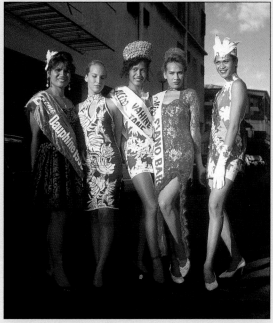

A young boy may adopt the female role by his own choice or that of his parents, performing female tasks at home and eventually finding a job usually performed by women, such as waiting on tables in a restaurant, making rooms in a hotel, or working as a bartender. Usually only one mahu exists in each village or community, evidence that the mahu serves a certain sociological function.

Though Tahitians may poke fun at mahus, they are fully accepted in society, some even teaching Sunday school. Many, but not all, mahus are homosexual. Today, some clubs in Papeete feature striptease by mahus, and some transvestites also engage in prostitution. The term *raerae* has been coined to describe male prostitutes. They even have special beauty contests, such as Miss Raerae or Miss Tane (the Tahitian word for "man").

sites. Most families treated their daughters little better than cattle, offering them to the sailors as welcome gifts. These old perceptions survive in the large number of rapes committed in Tahiti. Sexual violence is the second highest crime in Tahiti, and Polynesian society still views it with a certain ambivalence. In general, however, Tahitian men show a respectful attitude toward women. Male–female greetings in public are usually limited to a smile and a "hello" or wave.

Today's vahine has much more equality with men. Tahitian women are given the same educational opportunities as men, and they work as teachers, scientists, and truck drivers.

RELIGION

ALTHOUGH TAHITI IS A TERRITORY of France, where the main religion is Roman Catholicism, the majority of Tahitians are Protestants of the Evangelical Church. This is because the first Europeans to settle on the island were Protestant missionaries from the London Missionary Society. After an unsuccessful early attempt, Catholic missionaries arrived 39 years after the Protestant missionaries, and the Mormons followed eight years later. Today, aside from the Evangelical, Catholic, and Mormon churches, Seventh-Day Adventists, Jehovah's Witnesses, and Sanitos are also represented in Tahiti. A few Chinese are Buddhists.

The population of Tahiti is deeply religious, despite decades of secular living. Church attendance is very high, and many children attend schools run by the churches. In the outer islands, priests and local ministers wield considerable influence. Although the government recognizes no official religion, members of the Territorial Assembly say a few collective prayers before the start of the session.

Prior to the introduction of Christianity at the end of the 18th century, Tahitians had their own ancient religion. They believed in the immortality of the soul, in a heavenly paradise, and in reincarnation as another creature "on land, in the sea, or in the skies." When King Pomare II became Christian, many sacred statues and other religious symbols were destroyed. The conversion to Christianity was total, and there are no followers of the ancient religion today.

Opposite: **A Protestant church on Rangiroa.**

Below: **Attending church is a community event.**

THE EVANGELICAL CHURCH

More than half the population of Tahiti is Protestant. The first missionaries from the London Missionary Society arrived in 1797. Made up of Presbyterians, Methodists, Episcopalians, and Independentists, the mission did not encounter any success until 1812, when King Pomare II, for strategic reasons, converted to the new faith. Thereafter all Tahitians became Christians and the Pomare rulers staunchly upheld their faith. So influential were the Evangelical missionaries that one of them, George Pritchard, tried to convince Queen Pomare IV to ask the English king to make Tahiti a British protectorate. This started the conflict with the French that led to the eventual annexation of Tahiti by France.

White dresses, white straw hats, and formal suits are typical of the attire worn by those attending a Tahitian church service.

A CHURCH WITH A SOCIAL CONSCIENCE

The Evangelical Church actively promotes the improvement of the Tahitian people. To do so, it runs several schools that were models of education well before the first government school was built. Evangelical schools offer a secular education, in line with the government's policy, and are open to children of all faiths. Instead of teaching religious precepts, they put more emphasis on the personality of the students and their sense of responsibility.

The Church itself shoulders its fair share of social responsibility through its youth movements and rehabilitation centers. Its leaders are very outspoken on social issues, and have stated their opposition to nuclear testing on many occasions. They are always willing to meet government officials to discuss problems facing Tahitian society, such as inflation, pollution, and alcoholism. The Evangelical Church takes its role as pastoral guide seriously.

One of the most interesting churches is that of Mataiea, which was faithfully copied from a postcard depicting a Muslim mosque!

The Tahitian population was initially very hostile to Christianity, yet there were many similarities between their traditional religion and the Christian faith: *Maohi* legends that resemble Biblical stories; the existence of a God, creator of the universe; and the belief in an immortal soul. Once the first reticence was over, these similarities must have facilitated the implantation of Christianity in Tahiti.

Today's Evangelical Church is independent, looking solely to the Bible for guidance. The Church is organized into 27 parishes, each led by a pastor and a council of deacons. The parish itself comprises different pastoral groups with a deacon at the head. Each group is entrusted with various tasks within the community. In addition to the church building, there is also a parish house which acts as a meeting place for the congregation. Sunday school is conducted in this building. The most important church is that of Paofai in Papeete.

Sunday services are well attended, with most parishioners dressed smartly in white. All women wear a modernized version of the mission dress and white hats. Services are conducted in Tahitian and take up to two hours. The whole congregation joins the choir in singing beautiful hymns.

The first Catholic missionaries were poor gardeners, and of the many plants they brought, only the grapevine survived. The Tahitians tasted the grapes before they were ripe, and thinking the grapes were poisonous, they uprooted all the vines.

THE CATHOLIC CHURCH

The first attempt at converting the Tahitians to Catholicism took place in 1774, when two Franciscan priests were left on the island to spread the faith. They were so fainthearted that the mission failed dismally. Mistaking the curiosity of the natives for aggression, they locked themselves up in the mission and concluded that Tahiti was too dangerous for them. They went back to Peru one year later, leaving no trace of their passage.

The next Catholic missionaries arrived from France in 1834 but were sent away by Queen Pomare, upon the advice of the British missionary and consul Pritchard. It was not until the French established the protectorate that the Catholic Church gained more influence.

Today, half of the people in northern Tahiti are Catholic—mainly the Popaa government workers. They are concentrated in the urban region between Paea and Mahina, where most French expatriates live. (For this reason also, the Tuamotus, which shelter large numbers of French soldiers and officials working for the CEP, are overwhelmingly Catholic.)

The Catholic Church is very influential in the field of social services. It runs 17 primary schools and secondary schools and colleges in Tahiti. One of the largest is the Anne-Marie Javouhey college in Papeete, which has nearly 1,000 students. The Church is also active in the formation and running of youth organizations, including the Boy Scouts and the Sporting and Cultural Federation of France. In addition, the Church conducts family planning classes, organizes counseling sessions for families, and prepares young people for married life. The use of the media is vital for the Church to reach as many people as possible. Two Catholic newspapers are published, a bimonthly in French and a monthly paper in Tahitian. The Tepano Jaussen Center also prepares radio and television programs.

There are 34 Catholic churches in Tahiti, most of them in the urban

A Catholic church in Taravao.

sprawl of Papeete. The oldest and most important is Notre Dame Cathedral, built in 1875. Many new church buildings reflect modern architectural trends. The Saint Etienne Church in Punaauia has an interesting facade of overlapping triangles. Services are usually conducted in French and are characterized by immense fervor and beautiful singing.

THE LONGEST TEMPLE IN THE WORLD

After King Pomare II became a Christian, he decided to emulate the Biblical King Solomon and build a temple larger than that of Jerusalem.

Knowing nothing about Hebrew or European architecture, he based his temple on a traditional oval hut, using native timber and palm leaves. This method of construction enabled the temple to be built in less than a year. The central roof ridge rested on 36 pillars made of full-length breadfruit trees, and the lower edges of the roof rested on 280 shorter pillars of the same material. The walls, straight on the long sides but circular at the short ends, were made of sawn planks. The roof was covered with pandanus leaves.

Called the Royal Mission Chapel, the temple was 712 feet (217 m) long. However, due to the insufficiency of building materials and construction techniques, the width was only 54 feet (16 m) and the height 18 feet (5 m). By comparison, Saint Peter's Basilica in Rome is 616 feet (188 m) long, 379 feet (115 m) wide and 151 feet (46 m) high (without the cupola). The Royal Mission Chapel had 29 doors and 133 windows with sliding shutters to let in air and light. Because of its strange proportions, it looked more like a huge, flattened cowshed than the awe-inspiring monument that its builder intended it to be.

The corridor-shaped building could accommodate a congregation of 6,000 people, as happened once or twice a year during the general church assemblies. However, no preacher could make himself heard by everyone. This problem was solved by the erection of three pulpits: the first in the eastern nave, where the king sat with his nobles on wooden benches, the second in the middle, and the third in the western nave, where the commoners sat on a layer of dry grass spread out on the floor. The separation of the social classes was facilitated by a natural obstacle: a 5-foot- (1.5-m-) wide river, which the builders had not been able to divert, flowing diagonally across the floor.

With the death of Pomare II in 1821, the Royal Mission Chapel began to decay. It was eventually replaced by a wooden church of more manageable size, which was torn down at the end of the last century to make way for a charming 12-sided chapel. This was replaced by a slightly larger one in 1978.

This unusual shrine to the
Virgin Mary is inset with
sea shells.

OTHER CHURCHES

Five minor churches are active in Tahiti: the Church of Jesus Christ of
Latter-day Saints (Mormons), Reorganized Church of Jesus Christ of Latter-
day Saints (Sanitos), Seventh-Day Adventists, Jehovah's Witnesses, and the
Pentecostal Movement. Young Mormon missionaries continue to flock to
Tahiti from the United States for two-year stays. They travel in pairs and
are easily recognizable by their attire: short-sleeved white shirts with a tie.
All five churches are characterized by the payment of tithes and their
rejection of the established churches.

The Mormons, Sanitos, and Seventh-Day Adventists run their own
schools and organize activities for young people and women. Emphasis
is placed on the family, and training is considered important to improve
oneself economically. The Jehovah's Witnesses and Pentecostals do not
have much of a social agenda. Growing dissatisfaction with the established
churches coupled with the proselytizing efforts of the minor churches
ensure a growing influence for these churches.

This young woman wears a gold cross around her neck with her traditional Polynesian dress. The ancient Polynesian religion has disappeared from Tahiti forever.

POLYNESIAN FAITH

The ancient Polynesian world was peopled with gods, demigods, spirits, and elves, who could move freely between this world and theirs. The gods were represented by carved figures called *tiki* ("tee-KEE"). The spiritual power of the gods rested in the *mana* ("mah-NAH"), the essence of divine authority with which high chiefs were also endowed.

The most important place of worship was the *marae* ("mah-RAH-ay"), a rectangular area covered with paving stones and surrounded by low walls. The altar, in the form of a step pyramid, stood at one end. Worshipers asked for the gods' blessings by making offerings of fruits, vegetables, fish, pigs, and dogs, which were placed on wooden platforms. Once the gods had sampled each food, the priests carrying out the ceremony consumed the rest.

Human sacrifices were carried out in times of great crisis. Only men could be sacrificed, as women were considered impure and not worthy of the gods. The victim was ambushed and killed elsewhere before being offered to the gods.

Many restrictions, called *tapu* (the origin of the English word, taboo), were observed. Although Tahitians have been Christians for almost 200 years, many are still wary of going too close to the ancient places of worship.

The mythic themes of Polynesian religion helped to justify rank and social stratification to a people concerned with genealogy, respect and disrespect, and aspects of nature that needed to be explained and appeased. The Polynesian religion was an outgrowth of the Polynesian social structure, which focused on genealogical connections and the integration of the gods with nature and the human condition.

THE CREATION OF THE WORLD

According to the ancient Tahitians, a great octopus held the sky and earth together in its arms. The god Taaroa existed in the darkness of contemplation, and from this darkness he called the other gods into being. When Taaroa shook himself, feathers fell and turned into trees, plantains, and other green plants. Rua (the Abyss) killed the octopus by a magic trick, but it did not release its hold on the universe, and the demigods Ru, Hina, and Maui were born in the darkness. Ru raised the sky as high as the coral tree, but ruptured himself so that his intestines floated away to become the clouds that usually hang over the island of Bora Bora. Maui, the trickster, then used wedges to support the sky and went to enlist the help of Tane, who lived in the highest heaven. Tane drilled into the sky with a shell until light came through. The arms of the octopus fell away and became the island of Tubuai. Tane then decorated the sky with stars and set the sun and moon on their courses. The fish and sea creatures were given places and duties, and the god Tohu was given the job of painting the beautiful color on the fish and shells of the deep. In Tahiti, Tane was symbolized by a piece of finely braided coconut-fiber rope.

LANGUAGE

TAHITI HAS TWO OFFICIAL LANGUAGES: Tahitian and French. Official documents and speeches are generally in French and are rarely translated. Most people are fluent in French, although some low-income Polynesians speak only Tahitian. Many of the expatriate civil servants, on the other hand, do not understand the local language.

English is taught as a third language in some secondary schools, and many educated Demis and Chinese can speak it quite well. Most people employed in the tourist industry can manage a simple conversation in English. Large Chinese stores also have someone who can speak English, although the Chinese use the Hakka dialect among themselves.

Opposite: **French is the language of instruction in Tahitian schools.**

TAHITIAN PRONUNCIATION

Consonants
f   as in four
h   as in home, except when it is preceded by *i* and followed by *o* or *u*; then it sounds like *sh*
m   as in man
n   as in nine
p   as in super, while blowing as little air as possible
r   a rolled sound produced by caving in the tip of the tongue, closer to French
t   as in paste, with no explosion of air
v   as in vain, but sometimes also pronounced like a *w* or almost like a *b* with both lips touching
In some words, *r* and *n* are used interchangeably; *f* and *h* are also used as variants of each other.

Vowels
a   as in ah
e   as in pay
i   as in till
o   as in hose
u   as in good
Long vowels are the same as above, but pronounced as if they were doubled.

THE TAHITIAN LANGUAGE

Tahitian is one of a family of Austronesian languages spoken from Madagascar in the Indian Ocean through Indonesia, all the way to Easter Island and Hawaii. Among Polynesian languages, those of Eastern Polynesia and New Zealand (Tahitian, Hawaiian, Maori) are quite different from those of Western Polynesia (Samoan and Tongan). Within French Polynesia, the Tahitian language is spoken mainly in the Society Islands. However, as communications improve and the dominance of Tahiti over the rest of the territory grows, the dialects in the outer islands are more and more influenced by Tahitian.

There are eight consonants in Tahitian (*f, h, m, n, p, r, t, v*) and five vowels (*a, e, i, o, u*). Vowels can either be long or short. The small number of letters means that many words are spelled the same way, the difference in meaning given only by the length of the vowel. One interesting feature of Tahitian words is the sequence of two or three consecutive vowels, sometimes the same vowel (as in Faaa). Each vowel is pronounced separately, except for *ai, au, ae,* and *oi,* which are usually pronounced as diphthongs. There are no sequences of two consonants. An important sound in the Tahitian language is the glottal stop, which usually separates two vowel sounds. The glottal stop is produced by raising the back of the mouth to block the flow of air before pronouncing the next vowel. Two words spelled the

Studying a book on Tahitian grammar.

same way can be differentiated by the use of the glottal stop. In written texts, it is sometimes represented by an apostrophe.

A sentence is made up of the verb, the subject, and the object, in this order. Nouns do not have singular and plural forms, nor gender. To denote the plural, the word *mau* ("mah-OO") is added before the noun. To denote the masculine, the word *tane* ("tah-NAY," man) follows the noun while the word *vahine* (woman) following the noun means that it is a feminine word.

Just like any other living language, Tahitian is constantly changing. The influence of English is evident in the following words: *faraipani* (frying pan), *moni* (money), *painapo* (pineapple), *tapitana* (captain).

The Tahitian language had no written form until the first missionaries set about recording it. History, customs, and traditions were passed down from one generation to the next by word of mouth.

> *"The sad, weird, mysterious utterances of nature: the scarcely articulate stirrings of fancy . . . Faa-fano: the departure of the soul at death. Aa: happiness, earth, sky, paradise. Mahoi: essence or soul of God. Tapetape: the line where the sea grows deep. Tutai: red clouds on the horizon. Ari: depth, emptiness, a wave of the sea. Po: night, unknown dark world, Hell."*
>
> —Pierre Loti on the mystical vocabulary of Tahitian

A 20th-century tiki livens up the side of this phone booth.

TAHITIAN NAMES

In Tahitian society, a person's name is of utmost importance, because it confers certain qualities on its bearer. An inanimate object, such as a musical instrument, may also be given a name in order to confer spiritual qualities on it.

In pre-Christian times, the chiefs' names were supposed to contain supernatural power that was beneficial to their descendants but brought a curse on their usurpers. The chiefs could also take on a name to mark an important event. In this way, Tu, the first king of Tahiti, became Pomare after he visited his son who was sick with coughing. The words *po* (night) and *mare* (cough) became taboo since they were the king's name, and new words came into being to denote night and cough.

There were no surnames in ancient Tahiti. The nobles used the name of their marae to denote their association with a certain clan. However, all Tahitian families now have surnames.

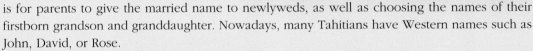

An ancient custom that is still in use today is for parents to give the married name to newlyweds, as well as choosing the names of their firstborn grandson and granddaughter. Nowadays, many Tahitians have Western names such as John, David, or Rose.

Tahitian names are actually part of a phrase with a certain meaning. Some of them are descriptive of the qualities invested in the bearer, while others refer more to a state of being. Here are a few examples:

Eeva (f) from Te-fetu-eeva-i-te-po, meaning "The star that rises at night."

Marotea (m) from Te-aito-maro-tea, meaning "The hero with a white belt."

Moetu (f) from Moe-tu-i-te-ara-nui, meaning "Asleep standing on the highway."

Viritua (m) from Viri-tua-i-te-moana-tapu, meaning "Rolling beyond the sacred sea."

FRENCH

In Tahiti, French is not seen as having more prestige than Tahitian. Its usage depends more on the educational level of the speaker than on his or her ethnic background. Demis families, having had access to education for several generations, are very fluent in both languages. French is used at home and on social occasions. Tahitian is reserved for conversations with Polynesians who are not very comfortable with French. The poor Demis families in rural areas, however, use Tahitian as their first language.

French is the working language in Papeete. In general, all official matters are conducted in it. And, of course, school is taught in French. The Tahitians speak French with a flourish, giving it a special richness with their rolled *R*s.

This colorful sign, written in French and Tahitian, promotes an anti-litter campaign.

Tahiti has a minor export industry in the production of postage stamps. Although the quality of the graphics and production has tended to be uneven, they are now in demand among overseas collectors. Stamps also serve as advertising for Tahiti.

NEWSPAPERS

The press in Tahiti has a very short history. The first newspaper, *Les Nouvelles de Tahiti*, hit the newsstands in 1957. Today the daily readership of 25,000 is split between *Nouvelles* and *La Dépêche de Tahiti*, which was first published in 1964. Both papers are in French and come out in the morning. *La Dépêche* is larger, with more international news. In 1989, the previously locally owned *Nouvelles* was purchased by French publishing magnate Robert Hersant, who also owns *La Dépêche*.

Both dailies publish news of general interest, including politics, current affairs, sports, and entertainment. Coverage of local news and events is quite comprehensive, although the newspapers are now devoting more space to the outer islands and the Pacific region. Reporting is usually free and independent, but both papers tend to be pro-French.

A free weekly newspaper is published in English. It is targeted at the tourist market and covers only news that is relevant to tourists. There is also an English magazine, the monthly *Tahiti Sun Press*. There is no national newspaper in Tahitian.

RADIO AND TELEVISION

Radio operations started in 1935 with a small group of amateur wireless operators broadcasting news and entertainment after 6 p.m. every day. The first radio station, Radio Tahiti – La Voix de France, was established in 1949, with programs in French and Tahitian. It has now been absorbed by the state-controlled RFO (Radio France d'Outre-Mer), which also broadcasts in the other French overseas departments and territories. The aim of RFO is to educate and reach out to as many listeners as possible. Its programs cater to every socioeconomic segment of the population and

Reading *Les Nouvelles de Tahiti* in a Papeete café.

to every ethnic group. In addition to RFO, nine private radio stations also operate in Tahiti. As these are commercial ventures, they tend to target specific sections of the population, such as young people or the Popaa community. Most of them play foreign music—English rock and pop and French pop music in particular.

RFO also operates two television stations in Tahiti, one in French and the other in Tahitian. Most of the programs are imported from three main stations in France and consist of current affairs programs, variety and game shows, and movies. American soap operas dubbed in French are very popular. Local television productions cover only local events and news. There is no private television station yet. Television is the most popular medium in Tahiti and each family owns at least one television set, spending most of their free time in front of it.

ARTS

THE ARTS SCENE IN TAHITI has been dominated by a few European personalities. Yet Tahitians are an innately artistic people who treasure beauty in their daily lives, as demonstrated by the flower garlands and headdresses they love to weave and wear. Artistry is displayed in every small garden plot, where flowers are grown in harmonious beauty. Local Tahitian artists have produced noteworthy works of art. Unfortunately, they are still overshadowed by the European artists of old.

However, it is in the performing arts that Tahiti really comes into its own. Tahitian dancing has been elevated to a precise art form, and standards keep improving, with regular dancing competitions that are hotly contested. One should hope that as Tahitian society becomes more familar to the rest of the world, other forms of artistic expression will gain as much recognition as dancing.

Opposite: **Making head-dresses and garlands from palm leaves and flowers is a very popular craft.**

Left: **Polynesian tattoos are striking and skilful. The traditional designs retain their popularity among Tahitian men.**

DANCING

The Tahitian term for dancing is *ori Tahiti* ("oh-REE tah-hih-TIH"), which means "Tahitian dancing in the traditional style." Another word commonly used to describe it is *tamure* ("tah-MOO-ray").

Tahitian children are exposed to dancing from a young age. Most schools teach dancing as a recreational activity, and local parishes also have their own dance groups where children are introduced to this ancient art form. Whereas the first missionaries viewed Tahitian dancing as obscene and sinful, the churches now promote it as a form of collective activity. Dance groups are formed at various levels, in church or in regional groups. Tamure is almost exclusively dancing in a group. Even though a dance may include a solo performance, it is the group movements that create the beauty of the dance.

Vivid and colorful costumes add to the visual effect of a dance. There are basically two types of costumes: *more* ("moh-RAY"), which is a grass skirt, and pareu, the colorful length of cotton. The more is the more elaborate costume. It is accompanied by a belt sewn with shells, flowers

PROFESSIONAL DANCE TROUPES

Until World War II, Tahitian dancing was considered immoral and was thus suppressed. Soon after the war, Madeleine Moua, an accomplished dancer, decided to give more dignity to dancing by forming the dance group Heiva in Papeete. Heiva was the first professional dance group in Tahiti, and the group is still very active. Today there are several professional troupes in the country, each with 20 to 40 members. Normal performances, however, do not require more than eight women and four men dancers. Most professional dancers are around 20 years old. Physical requisites for men are average size, at least shoulder length hair, and no beard or mustache. Women dancers should have a slim and graceful silhouette, a pleasant face, and long, dark hair. Height and size are important in tamure because group dancing requires uniformity.

and seeds, a garland of flowers or shells, a flower headdress, and a bra for the women dancers. Women sling the more low on the hips to accentuate the hip movements, while male dancers tie theirs at the waist. For special events, the flower headdress is replaced by a tall elaborate headgear made of fibers, and men dancers add a short cape to the costume. Dancers also hold in their hands a tuft of fibers like longish pompoms, called *ii*. The pareu, on the other hand, is worn with only a garland and flowers in the hair.

Four types of dances are performed in Tahiti today: *otea, aparima, hivinau,* and *paoa*. The most well-known and ancient is the *otea*, and Tahitians look upon it as a symbol of their culture.

Amateur or professional, Tahitians love to dance.

OTEA *Otea* ("oh-TAY-ah") is performed for special events. For this reason, the dancers always wear the more. The larger the group of dancers, the more beautiful it is. *Otea* can bring together up to 60 dancers, and the minimum is six. The dancers form separate columns of men and women facing the spectators. They all move at the same time, and the formation remains the same throughout the performance. Otea is physically very demanding and does not last more than six minutes. A performance usually consists of a series of otea lasting 15 minutes. When otea is danced by a group of men, it is a war dance and the dancers often hold a spear in their hands.

APARIMA *Aparima* ("AH-pah-ree-mah") is a narrative dance that is sometimes accompanied by a song. Dressed in pareu, the dancers are placed in the same column formation as for otea. At least six men and

Tahitian children learn to dance from a young age. Their movements and costumes are the same as those of adult dancers.

women are required for this dance. Depicting scenes from daily life, such as fishing or preparing food, the dancers use their hands to mime their actions. The emphasis is placed on the hand movements, and the aparima is usually performed in a kneeling position or in a sitting position with legs tucked underneath.

HIVINAU *Hivinau* ("hee-vee-NOW") comes from the English term "heave now" used by the 19th-century English-speaking sailors when lifting anchor. It is essentially a party dance, and children and old people can also join in. When performed for an audience, hivinau brings together a mixed group of around 20 male and female dancers dressed in more. The dancers form two circles, men and women separately, with a singer and a group of musicians in the middle. The two circles are in constant motion, moving in opposite directions or both in a clockwise direction. The male singer sings a few lines and the dancers answer with *Ahiri a ha ahaha!* This phrase does not have any meaning—it is only a shout of joy. A common subject for hivinau is fishing and the sea.

PAOA *Paoa* ("pah-OH-ah") originates from the tapa-making sessions, when a group of women sat down to beat tree bark into tapa cloth, singing and beating at the same time. Today, the subject of the dance is usually fishing or hunting. The paoa dance group consists of a male singer, a large choral group of men and women, musicians, and one or two dancers. Depending on the occasion, the group wears more or everyday clothes.

90

These men are dancing at the Heiva i Tahiti festival. Such dramatic costumes are only worn for special events.

BASIC TAMURE MOVEMENTS

The basic step for men is the *paoti* ("PAH-oh-tih"). The legs are held close together with heels touching, feet pointing outward, and knees slightly bent. The knees then move outward and inward in a scissors motion while the heels come up slightly. Arms are stretched out horizontally, with the elbows straight and fingers held together and pointing slightly upward. The rest of the body does not move at all.

For women, the starting position is the same as for men. The knees are then slightly raised, alternating between left and right, as if walking on the spot. Since the heels are still flat on the ground, this knee movement causes the hips to swing out from side to side. They are not supposed to twist forward. Arms are outstretched, as for men. It is essential that the shoulders and upper torso do not move.

PAINTING

Almost right from the moment Tahiti was discovered, the island was the subject of painting by Europeans who wanted to record its landscapes and people. The first painter to depict scenes of Tahiti was Englishman William Hodges, who was part of Cook's second expedition in 1773. He made pictorial records of the ships' landing and scenes of daily life, and drew portraits of the Tahitian people, including Omai and King Pomare. The 19th century attracted more painters in search of inspiration. While Frenchmen Paul Gauguin and Jacques Boullaire were more interested in painting faces and expressions, Englishwoman C.F. Gordon Cumming painted beautiful watercolors depicting Papeete and other Tahitian landscapes.

Tahitian painting today is no longer the domain of foreigners in search of exoticism. Several local painters have made a name for themselves through regular exhibitions, and an Association of Artists was created in 1984 to develop this art form. One of the most well-known Tahitian painters is Ruy Juventin, who actively promotes local painting. Since there is no tradition of painting in Tahitian society, artists tend to follow European models, and there are a variety of styles in their productions.

PAUL GAUGUIN

Paul Gauguin was in a desperate financial situation when he arrived in Tahiti in 1891. He started out by painting the portraits of wealthy settlers in Papeete, but he soon grew tired of this and left Papeete for Mataiea.

It was in Mataiea that Gauguin painted his most famous canvases. He lived with a young vahine named Tehaamana, who was one of his favorite models. In this two-year period he produced 66 paintings, among them such masterpieces as *Ia Orana Maria, Hina Tefatou, Manao tupapau, Fatata te miti, Rêverie,* and *Under the Pandanus.*

Gauguin left Tahiti in 1893, hoping to sell his paintings in Paris. However, his exhibition of paintings of Tahitians caused a scandal. Then he started writing a book entitled *Noa Noa*, in which he described life in Tahiti as a blissful existence. He returned to Tahiti in 1895, but he was plagued by financial and health problems, and his painting took on a more pensive note. He died in the Marquesas in 1903, in abject poverty.

During his lifetime, Gauguin was treated harshly by the French government and settlers, and redress did not come until 1965, when the Gauguin Museum was opened in Papeari. The museum reconstructs Gauguin's life in Tahiti with the help of photographs and other objects. Unfortunately, very few original paintings are displayed, since most of the painter's works are now displayed at famous museums around the world.

"Before very long I am going to Tahiti. It's a little island in the Pacific where you can live without having to worry about money. I want to forget all the bad things that have happened and die over there without anyone here knowing. I want to be free to paint, as I am not interested in having a glorious reputation."

—*Paul Gauguin*

LITERATURE

Just like painting, writing about Tahiti has traditionally come from European and American authors. The first piece of writing about Tahiti was Bougainville's myth-making account of his visit to the island. About a century later, Pierre Loti (whose real name was Louis-Marie Julien Viaud) wrote *Le Mariage de Loti*, a sad love story between a young French navy lieutenant and a teenage vahine. The book was an instant success. Tahiti has also inspired much writing in English, including novels by Herman Melville (*Typee* and *Omoo*) and poetry by Rupert Brooke (*Tiare Tahiti*).

Literature in the Tahitian language only started in the 1960s. It was written mainly by intellectuals in search of their cultural identity. Duro Raapoto is a linguist, poet, and fervent defender of the Tahitian language. His poems deal with the difficulties of life and reveal the aspirations of the Polynesian people. John Mairai uses theater to claim his Polynesian identity. His plays deal with the problems of daily life, and his caustic dialogues go down very well with his Tahitian audiences.

CARVING

Ancient Tahitians carved plain, realistic figures, either as statues or as ornaments. Tiki are wooden or stone statues that had a religious significance. Petroglyphs are scenes carved out of stone, depicting stylized characters such as fish, turtles, or headdresses. Articles for daily use or ornamental purposes were sculpted into decorative designs. Combs, handles of fans, and bowls were intricately carved out of wood, basalt, bone, and shell.

Today's artists still use the same materials. Precious woods like sandalwood, rosewood and *tou* ("toh-OO") are carved into weapons, tiki, and flat dishes. Basalt stone is best for pestles and adzes.

There are a number of other crafts to be found in Tahiti. Tahiti is well-known for its basket work. Pandanus leaves are woven into hats, baskets, and mats. Tahitian artisans are experts at making flower garlands and headdresses. Shells and coral are made into beautifully intricate jewelry.

Although their features are stylized, Polynesian carvings can be very expressive.

PATCHWORK QUILTS

An interesting craft in Tahiti is the two-layer patchwork quilt called *tifaifai* ("tih-FAI-fai"). Made of light cotton, it is the local adaptation of the quilting art taught by missionaries. In the tifaifai, one large design is appliquéd onto the cotton base in bold color combinations, producing an unmistakable Tahitian look. Floral patterns and contrasting colors are preferred. The quilt is used to cloak newlyweds and cover coffins. A good one takes up to six months to complete. Tifaifai-making is solely the domain of women, and each woman has individual quilt patterns that are her trademarks. French painter Henri Matisse, who spent several weeks in Papeete, was so impressed by the tifaifai designs that he applied the same technique and adopted many designs for his paintings.

LEISURE

TAHITIANS BELIEVE THAT WORK is a necessary evil that must be done so that they can afford to enjoy themselves during their leisure time. They do not desire to gain more material wealth if they have to sacrifice their leisure activities for it.

Sports, dancing, and having fun play an important part in the Tahitians' daily lives. They prefer leisure activities that involve a group of people because Tahitian society was traditionally one of communal living. Getting together with a group of *fetii* ("fay-tee-EE"), even if only for a chat, is a source of great enjoyment. *Fetii* means "relatives," but the word is commonly used in a wider sense of "close friends."

Together with these traditional activities, Tahitians spend a lot of time performing a very modern activity: watching television.

In many areas, especially in the countryside, a person's leisure time is dominated by church-related activities. Members of the choir get together for rehearsals, while others form committees to organize social gatherings such as celebratory dinners or dancing parties.

Left: **A relaxing game of pool.**

Opposite: **Tahitians love water sports, both as participants and as spectators.**

String instruments such as the guitar and ukulele are an imported tradition. There are two local versions of the ukulele. One is a piece of wood glued to half a coconut shell. The other is carved from a piece of wood with a length of goatskin covering the opening. Both have four nylon strings.

A himene group performs at a hospital on Tiare Tahiti Day.

MUSIC

Music is in the blood of the Tahitian people. At home after work, they bring out a guitar or ukulele and sing a few songs. Groups of fetii meet on the weekend to sing and make music. Although they also play traditional Tahitian ballads, they prefer English pop songs. Nowadays, it is common to bring along a portable stereo which provides the music while everyone sings along, chats, or drinks. No party or outing is complete without music.

Singing in Tahitian is called *himene* ("hee-MAY-nay"), from the English word "hymn." Indeed, the church is where most of the singing activity takes place. However, the word also refers to any form of group singing. Himene groups are usually formed on a regional basis, and anyone, young or old, can be a member. Singing is done while seated, with a male soloist leading the group. *Himene tarava* ("hee-MAY-nay tah-RAH-vah") consists of a large number of men and women singing *a capella* (without instrumental accompaniment) in six to 10 parts. It narrates ancient Tahitian legends or historical events. *Ute* ("OO-tay") is less dignified: a group of men and women sing a refrain in a guttural voice while a soloist improvises a comic or satirical narration.

Himene groups also take part in some dances, like aparima and hivinau. On these occasions, they sing to the accompaniment of musical instruments.

TAHITIAN DRUMS

The traditional Tahitian musical instrument is the drum. *Toere* ("toh-AY-ray") is an unusual drum carved out of one piece of wood. It is basically a hollowed-out tree trunk with a rectangular slit running down the middle. The drummer holds it upright with one end on the floor and beats the side with a stick to produce a staccato beat. Toere come in three sizes, and each size produces a different sound. Some musicians give a name to their toere in order to impart certain spiritual qualities to it or to distinguish it from others by the sound it produces.

Faatete ("fah-AH-tay-tay") is another ancient drum. It is made from a hollowed tree trunk covered with a skin, traditionally shark but today more commonly calf. The skin is stretched before each performance and loosened afterward. Faatete usually measure 25 inches (64 cm) in height and 12 inches (30 cm) in diameter. Decorative motifs are carved on the sides.

Pahu ("pah-HOO") is of Western origin and can be made from wood or cut out of a metal barrel. In order to produce quality sound, the diameter and height must be roughly the same, (20–30 inches or 51–76 cm). The covering is of calfskin, and the pahu is decorated with paintings. The drum has two skins, but only one side is beaten with a stick. The drummer sometimes uses his hand to hit the other side. The musician is always seated with the pahu on its side in front of him.

THE LURE OF WATER

Typical islanders, Tahitians love all activities related to water. Swimming is a favorite pastime, in rivers and the sea and under waterfalls. Picnics are very popular weekend outings because they combine family togetherness with the opportunity to go swimming. Favorite picnic places are the beach or an isolated motu.

Tahitians really come into their own when practicing water sports. Surfing is one of the most ancient activities in Tahiti, having been documented by the first European visitors. Tahitian children do not need to go to the expense of buying fancy surfboards. They can ride the waves with anything at hand, as long as it is flat and light. The French national champions for surfing and windsurfing are usually Tahitians, and French surfers and windsurfers find that Tahiti is the ideal location in which to prepare for international competitions. Canoeing is another ancient sport. Tahitian canoes require several people to row, testing the team's strength, endurance, and sense of timing.

SPORTS

The most popular sport is soccer. Well before the colonizers brought the game, the ancient Tahitians practiced a ball game called *tuiraa* ("too-ee-RAH-ah"), which consisted of kicking a ball into the opponent's camp. Competition was fierce between the districts, and it was as popular as soccer is today. Soccer matches take place on weeknights and weekends at two different locations: Fautaua Stadium or Stade Pater, both located in Pirae near Papeete. Enthusiastic crowds cheer on their favorite teams. Other team sports, such as volleyball and basketball, are also very popular, especially among the lower income groups. Games of *pétanque* ("pay-TAHNK," French bowling) take place in rural areas.

More expensive sports, practiced mainly by the wealthy Demis and Popaa, are tennis, golf, and horseback riding. Tennis courts are located mainly in the hotels and in Papeete. The Atimaono golf course was built on a former cotton plantation located between the lagoon and the mountains in a very colorful setting. There are two riding schools in Pirae, which organize excursions into the mountains and tropical forests.

Tahiti has a beautiful golf course flanked by mountains, but not all Tahitians can afford to play.

Local spectator sports include Tahitian-style horse racing and cockfighting. Jockeys ride bareback, dressed in a brightly colored pareu and a flower headdress. Races are held on special occasions at the Pirae Hippodrome. Cockfighting, on the other hand, is officially illegal. However, fighting rings are out in the open, and the cockfights draw large crowds. Both horse racing and cockfighting take place on Sunday afternoons.

Sport fishing for marlin, shark, and other big game attracts many visitors to Tahiti. One of the most famous was U.S. novelist Zane Grey, who made several fishing expeditions to Tahiti in the 1920s. His determination was rewarded by the capture of a 1,000-pound (454-kg) marlin in 1930.

GAMBLING

Tahitians of all social backgrounds like to gamble. Although there is no national lottery, tombolas organized by various groups year round are very popular. Large sums of money are risked, and the draw is eagerly awaited by all concerned. Horse racing also gives rise to betting through the official Pari-mutuel. Even though payoffs are quite small compared to the tombolas, betting on horse races is still popular. Serious betting is also done on the outcome of cockfights, although this is, of course, illegal.

Tahitians like to spend a day at the races, particularly if they can place a bet on their favorite horse!

Casino-style gambling takes place under the cover of charity evenings organized by the Lion's Club or other charitable organizations. Patrons play roulette and blackjack in a secretive atmosphere. Games of Asian origin, such as "big and small" or *van lak*, are also played, mostly illegally. Keno, a type of lotto, draws large crowds.

However, Tahitians do not need any betting structure to gamble. Many weekends are spent playing cards for cash wagers. The contests during Heiva i Tahiti give rise to the most widespread betting of the year.

LA BRINGUE

Bringue ("BRAING") means having a good time, drinking, singing, dancing. There is no specific activity called bringue. Weddings, parties, discos, and other celebrations are all bringue. Some rural districts organize their own Saturday night bringue, usually as a fundraising activity.

Stone fishing is a communal activity that is fast disappearing. Several canoes form a semicircle around a school of fish and the men beat the water with stones tied to ropes. The fish are driven toward the shore, where women and children catch them in the shallow waters.

The music and dancing at a bringue are most often of Western inspiration. Pop songs and disco-style dancing are the norm. Sometimes the songs are in Tahitian, but the music is Western. Tahitian music is also played and people dance, but the participants do not do the traditional tamure. With couples facing each other, the woman swings her hips and the man opens and closes his knees. Young and old have fun at the bringue. Children sing and dance with their parents and grandparents, and the bringue does not end until late into the night.

FESTIVALS

SURPRISINGLY FOR A COUNTRY whose population is so keen on having fun, Tahiti does not have many colorful festivals. Because of the far-reaching influence of the Evangelical Church, religious celebrations are marked with sobriety, and do not give rise to the carnivalesque festivities common on other islands.

The most remarkable festival is a political one, Heiva i Tahiti, which marks the country's accession to internal autonomy. The most popular activities during Heiva i Tahiti are the competitions of traditional and modern sports, dancing, and himene.

Tahiti has the same public holidays as France, but festivals include those of the other segments of the population, such as Chinese New Year and Tiare Tahiti Day, which honors Tahiti's national flower.

Above: **Getting into the spirit of the festival, this woman has decorated her hair with tiare flowers for Tiare Tahiti Day.**

Opposite: **Spectacular dance costumes are worn for the Heiva i Tahiti celebrations.**

CALENDAR OF FESTIVALS

January 1	New Year's Day
March 5	Missionaries Day
March–April	Good Friday
March–April	Easter Monday
May 1	May Day
May	Ascension Day
May–June	Whitsunday and Whitmonday
June 29	Internal Autonomy Day
July	Heiva i Tahiti
July 14	Bastille Day
August 15	Assumption Day
November 1	All Saints' Day
November 11	Armistice Day
December 25	Christmas

Dancers at Heiva i Tahiti.

HEIVA I TAHITI

The most important and colorful festival of the year is Heiva i Tahiti, which means simply "Festival of Tahiti." Festivities start on June 29, Internal Autonomy Day, and culminate on Bastille Day on July 14, cleverly linking two directly opposing inspirations, the nationalism of the Tahitian people and the colonial dominance of France. The festival comes from the French national day festivities during colonial times. While the governor and French administrators celebrated the occasion with a ball and state banquet, the Tahitians were entertained with traditional games and cultural performances. In 1984, when Tahiti was granted full internal autonomy, the pro-French president of the Territorial Assembly hit upon the idea of bringing the start of the festivities forward by a few days to June 29 and combining the internal autonomy celebrations with those of Bastille Day.

The highlights of the Heiva festivities are most certainly the various competitions pitting contestants from the different districts and from the outer islands. Traditional competitions are canoe racing, javelin throwing, stone lifting, coconut husking, basket weaving, and tamure and himene competitions. Canoe races for both men and women are fiercely contested, with teams coming from all over the world. The canoes are carved out of a single tree trunk, and the race covers 4 miles (6.5 km) along the Papeete waterfront. One unusual event is the fruit-bearers' race. Male participants, dressed in pareu and flower headdresses, carry a colorful load of tropical fruits balanced on two ends of a banana tree trunk over a distance of 1.25 miles (2 km).

Less exotic competitions include bicycle, car, and horse races, pétanque, and archery contests. Traditional tattooing sessions bring together young people who want to experience their cultural heritage. Bringues are organized by regional organizations, and there is much dancing and feasting.

The Heiva celebrations also give rise to a festival of artisans. Palm-covered booths are crammed with the crafts of Polynesia. This is the largest gathering of craftspeople in French Polynesia. Hundreds of artisans gather to exhibit their artistry. Special events are held, including demonstrations of tifaifai quilting, weaving, and flower headdress making. The artisans dress in traditional attire, and there is always music and dancing.

July 2nd, which falls during the Heiva festival, evokes a totally different sentiment. This is the anniversary of the first French nuclear test at Moruroa in 1966, and antinuclear protests take place in Papeete.

The fruit-bearers' race is one of the most popular races because it is always difficult to predict the winner. One year, a prisoner on special leave won the race!

BASTILLE DAY

Bastille Day on July 14 marks the end of the Heiva celebrations. France's national day, Bastille Day commemorates the storming of the Bastille prison on July 14, 1789, at the height of the French Revolution. It symbolizes the end of the tyranny of the kings and a new era of freedom and democracy for the French people.

In Tahiti, the streets are decorated with both the French and the Tahitian flag, and a military parade takes place in Papeete. Speeches are made, the Republic is toasted, and fireworks light up the night sky. An all-night ball, today's version of the Governor's Ball, attracts revelers on July 13 in Papeete.

Nowadays, the military parade is losing its importance. Since Tahiti gained internal autonomy, attention has focused more on the parades of sports and cultural associations, which bring together himene groups, tamure troupes, and Chinese dancers, all dressed in their best finery.

RELIGIOUS FESTIVALS

The major Christian holidays are celebrated with fervor in Tahiti. Every Tahitian Christian attends church service, and the himene singing is even more beautiful on such occasions.

Christmas is certainly the most important religious holiday. However, this is a tropical Christmas. Flowers are in full bloom, and they decorate houses and churches. Many church organizations hold a bringue with food cooked in a traditional buried oven. Children polish their shoes so *Père Noël* ("pair noh-ELL," Santa Claus) will leave presents in or on them.

Tahitians take special care of their relatives' graves on All Saints' Day, cleaning the graves and decorating them with flowers.

Easter is ushered in by a late-night vigil. Some Catholics fast for 40 days, the duration of Lent, a period when Christians get ready spiritually for the miracle of the resurrection. Mass is said on the three days preceding Easter, with reenactments of Jesus Christ's last actions before being crucified. Chocolate eggs and Easter bunnies are given to children.

On All Saints' Day, families spend the day cleaning the graves of all the cemeteries at Papeete, Faaa, Arue, and Punaauia and decorating them with flowers. Flower stands are set up all over the island, and people light candles in the cemetery.

Assumption Day is celebrated only by the Catholic community. It marks the assumption of the Virgin Mary to heaven. The church service pays special attention to children, for they are all considered children of Mary.

A special holiday in Tahiti is March 5, Missionaries Day or Gospel Day. It commemorates the arrival of Protestant missionaries in 1797. Protestant churches hold a special service.

Reflecting the Polynesians' love of music, the Night of the Guitar is a special fair when guitars and ukuleles are taken out to make music.

FAIRS

In addition to public holidays, there are a number of non-holiday fairs celebrating a flower or a region.

Taupiti O Papeete in May celebrates the town of Papeete. Miss Papeete is elected, and a carnival atmosphere reigns, with rides, games, and contests. The important activities take place on weekends.

The day honoring Tahiti's national flower, the *tiare Tahiti*, falls on December 2nd. A tiare flower is presented to everyone on the streets of Papeete, in the hotels, and at the airport. The highlight of this fair is an all-night ball with tiare flowers decorating the ballroom, the tables, and even the performers.

CHINESE NEW YEAR

The Chinese community of Tahiti, together with all other Chinese populations worldwide, celebrates Chinese New Year in January or February. Based on the lunar calendar, Chinese New Year marks the arrival of spring in China and is thus a time of new beginnings and of taking stock. The most important part of Chinese New Year is the reunion dinner on New Year's Eve. On this evening, the whole family gathers for a special dinner prepared with much care. Everyone makes it a point to be home early, and married children return to their parents' house for dinner. After the dinner, parents give *hong bao* ("hong POW," red envelopes containing money) to the children.

A number of cultural performances are staged to mark Chinese New Year. Dances and fireworks are always on the program. Chinese businesses, especially grocery stores, remain closed for several days, as this is the only occasion during the year when the shopkeeper can take time off.

BEAUTY CONTESTS

Throughout the year, there is a proliferation of beauty contests attracting the most beautiful girls in Tahiti. Most of the contestants are young and are tempted by the prizes offered and by the celebrity that comes with being elected Miss Tahiti or Miss Papeete.

Beauty queens are chosen to represent sports clubs, philanthropic associations, the Chinese community, and other groups. In addition, nightclubs in Papeete try to attract more customers by organizing regular beauty contests promoting a brand of beer or liquor or representing the nightclub. A Miss Heiva is elected in June, and she acts as a queen of the celebrations.

Male beauty contests are also common, and a Miss Raerae is chosen every year from the transvestite community.

FOOD

TAHITIAN CUISINE MAKES USE of what nature provides in profusion: fish, fruits, and vegetables. However, aside from the staples like breadfruit, taro, and bananas, most of the fruits and vegetables used in daily meals have been introduced in the last two centuries. Coconut milk is used to flavor sauces, and coconut cream turns desserts into something special.

As a rule, Tahitian food is bland. Some dishes, especially such delicacies as raw fish and *popoi* ("POH-poy"), are an acquired taste. Popoi, a paste made from breadfruit, used to be the mainstay of the Tahitian diet but has now been replaced by the long loaf of French bread. Polynesian, Popaa, and Chinese alike eat baguettes at every meal. The reasons are both practical and economic. Bread does not require any preparation, and it is one of the most filling and least expensive items of food available. A typical Tahitian breakfast consists of bread, coffee, and perhaps some fruit.

The main meal of the day for the Popaa population is lunch, consisting of meat, potatoes, and bread, sometimes accompanied by wine. Dinner is very light, usually leftovers from lunch. For the Polynesians and Chinese, on the other hand, dinner is the heaviest meal of the day.

Restaurants are plentiful in Papeete, offering French, American, Italian, Chinese, and Vietnamese cuisine. They tend to be very expensive—few Polynesians can afford to go out to a restaurant. Instead, Polynesians head for the lunch wagons near the harbor. These small vans appear at around 5:30 p.m., serving cheap and good plate dinners, kabobs, French fries, and grilled meats.

Opposite: **A juicy mango makes a delicious snack. Tahiti has many varieties of tropical fruit.**

Below: **Open throughout the night, wagons cater to bringue-goers.**

FISH

The favorite protein of Tahitians is fish. In fact, many families cannot afford meat; fish, on the other hand, is free and can be caught by anyone. About 300 species of fish abound in Polynesian waters, but not all of them are edible. The armored soldier fish and unicorn fish are prized by Tahitian gourmets. Sea bass and blue spotted grouper release a wonderful aroma when grilled, while parrotfish, Napoleon fish, and jacks are best eaten raw.

Fish is mainly prepared in three ways: poached, grilled, and raw. Poaching is an easy way of cooking fish. Lagoon fish such as red mullet, grouper, sea bass, and jacks are cooked in a clear broth and drizzled with coconut milk before serving. For grilling, Tahitians use coral as fuel, in addition to firewood. The fire is started with twigs and coconut husks, and small pieces of coral are placed on top. Once the coral is hot and has turned brownish, the fish are placed directly on them for cooking. Aside from lagoon fish, mahi mahi and tuna are also grilled.

However, one of the most popular ways to consume fish is to eat it raw. The more conventional dish is a type of salad that contains tomatoes, carrots, and onions. The fish, preferably fresh tuna, is first marinated in lime juice before being mixed with the salad vegetables and coconut milk. This dish is simply called *poisson cru* ("pwa-son CROO"), meaning "raw fish" in French.

Fafaru ("fah-fah-ROO") requires a more intriguing preparation, and the Tahitian people are divided over its merits. Those who like it love it, while those who dislike it hate it intensely. Three or four fish are placed in an airtight coconut-shell container and covered with sea water. The fish are left to soak in the water for two to three days, and then the liquid is sieved through a fine cloth before being returned to the container, while the fish are thrown away. Fresh fish cut into cubes is then added to the liquid and left to marinate for at least six hours before the fafaru is ready for consumption. The marinating liquid lends a very pungent aroma to the dish, and it is definitely an acquired taste. Raw fish is eaten on Sundays, special occasions, or when entertaining guests.

Opposite: **Fresh fish for sale at Papeete market.**

FISH POISONING

Ciguatera is a type of food poisoning resulting from the consumption of toxic tropical fish. The fish themselves are poisoned by the *Gambierdiscus toxicus* (G.T.) toxin, which is associated with algae growing on dead coral. The most frequently affected species are sea-perch, emperors, grouper, parrotfish, Napoleon fish, and triggerfish, which all unfortunately form part of the Tahitians' staple diet. Deep-sea fish such as tuna, bonito, and mahi mahi are never toxic. Every year around 1,000 people become victims of ciguatera in French Polynesia.

Ciguatera manifests itself in various symptoms, including a tingling sensation on the face and hands, vomiting, and diarrhea. The body feels weak, and the victim aches all over. Itching also occurs on the palms of the hands and the soles of feet, and for this reason, ciguatera is also known as "the itch." Severe cases can lead to death. However, normal cases of ciguatera are easily treated, and the symptoms subside after a few days.

Breadfruit paste wrapped in palm leaves.

The texture of cooked breadfruit resembles fresh bread rolled up into a semi-firm mass.

ALL-PURPOSE TREES

Called *uru* ("OO-roo") in Tahitian, the breadfruit is probably the most useful tree in Tahiti. Ancient Polynesian legends tell of a man who turned himself into a breadfruit tree to save his family from famine. A single tree can produce fruit three times a year for 50 years, with as many as 300 fruits each time. The starchy, easily digested fruit is rich in vitamin B and carbohydrates. In ancient times, to preserve the fruit for long voyages or to prevent famine, mashes were prepared; to make *mahi* ("mah-HEE"), fragments of pulp were cooked after they had been left to ferment in a trench covered with leaves and soil. The trunk of the breadfruit tree was hollowed into small outrigger canoes, the bark was beaten into tapa cloth, and the latex was used as a glue for capturing birds. The latex is still used today as a plaster for healing fractures, sprains, and rheumatic joints.

The coconut palm is another multipurpose tree. Like the breadfruit tree, it gives shade and decorates the landscape. The edible parts are the nut and the heart of the young sprout. The heart is very tender and can be eaten as a salad. The nut provides coconut water and coconut milk. The husk can be plaited or twisted into a rope and provides an ochre dye for all kinds of decoration. The flesh (copra), when dried, is squeezed for oil, which is used to make scented skin oil, perfumes, and soaps. The palm fronds are woven into mats, hats, baskets, and roofs. The ribs are used for making skewers and brooms. The trunk is sometimes used as building material, and the bark and roots become ingredients of traditional remedies.

STAPLES

The traditional staple foods in the Tahitian diet are breadfruit, taro, *fei* ("fay-EE") bananas, yam, and sweet potato. They are usually boiled or grilled and are eaten with fish and meats. Fei bananas are small, sweet, and red and must be cooked before being eaten.

Breadfruit is the most common staple. It is cooked whole over a wood fire, then peeled and eaten. A variation is to put the cooked breadfruit in a breadfruit leaf and hit it to form a paste. To eat, the breadfruit paste is dipped into warm coconut milk. Breadfruit is also used to prepare popoi, another type of mash. The fruit is grated, then wrapped in leaves before being boiled in water. Once cooked, the leaf is peeled off, lime juice and water are added, and the breadfruit is pounded for a while. Popoi is ready when the paste becomes elastic, and it is eaten with mashed bananas.

Tahitians enjoy a delicious desert called poe *("poh-AY"). It is a pudding made with tapioca flour and baked banana, papaya, or pumpkin. The flour and fruit are mixed with coconut cream and flavored with vanilla.*

Fresh fruit, vegetables, and seafood are readily available in Tahiti.

THE TAHITIAN OVEN

The equivalent of the Hawaiian *luau*, the Tahitian *ahimaa* ("ah-hee-MAH-ah") is reserved for feasts called *tamaaraa* ("tah-MAH-ah-RAH-ah") and can feed at least 30 people. More than a simple banquet, the preparation and eating of this feast is an exercise in communal living. Men dig the pit while women wrap the foods to be cooked.

The pit is 9 feet (2.7 m) long, 2 feet (61 cm) wide, and 1 foot (30 cm) deep. It is dug at around noon in order for the food to be ready by dinnertime. Dry branches and twigs are used to cover the bottom. Basalt stones are then placed on top of the branches, and a fire is lit in the pit. When the stones are red-hot, green branches and a layer of green banana leaves are spread over the stones, and the food is placed on top of the leaves. The whole pit is then covered with several layers of banana leaves, wet sacking, and sand. The ahimaa is left to bake for three hours.

Preparing an *ahimaa* with pork and breadfruit wrapped in palm leaves.

The foods that go into the oven are wrapped separately in banana leaves in order to retain their individual flavors: suckling pig, fish, lobster, shrimp, *fafa* ("fah-FAH," chopped bits of chicken cooked with the tops of taro greens and coconut milk), poe, breadfruit, sweet potato, taro, and fei bananas. Everything is eaten with the fingers off banana leaves, accompanied by a coconut-milk sauce fermented with the juice of river shrimp. In addition to the ahimaa, fafaru and popoi are also eaten at the tamaaraa. Drinks include beer, red wine, and water.

A tamaaraa is always accompanied by music. The band is usually made up of guitars, a ukelele, and a unique instrument made of a gasoline can tied to a broomstick with a piece of string. Participants wear flowers in their hair, and colorful flowers decorate the banquet table and surroundings. The tamaaraa is a perfect occasion for family and friends to gather in a convivial atmosphere.

FIRIFIRI

Firifiri is a donut in a figure-eight shape covered with icing sugar. It is sold at markets and roadside stalls and eaten for breakfast or as a snack with a cup of coffee.

3 cups flour
1 package dry yeast
1.5–2 cups water
1 cup sugar

Mix the flour and dry yeast. Add water and mix to form a soft dough. Add sugar to taste and leave to rise for 4–5 hours.

Cut the dough into pieces, pull them and twist to form the figure eight.

Fry in very hot peanut oil until golden.

Roll the firifiri in icing sugar.

TAHITIAN DRINKS

The ancient Tahitians used a rather interesting method to make an intoxicating drink. Fresh kava roots were chewed, usually by women, and the saliva-covered roots were diluted in water to produce a type of liquor.

Beer is the most popular drink. The traditional Tahitian beer was made with fruit juices (oranges or pineapples) to which water and sugar were added. It was bottled and left to ferment for 4–5 days, which caused the fizz in the drink. Today the local brewery produces a brand of European-style beer called Hinano from imported hops, malt, and yeast. Only the water is Tahitian. Beer is considered a social drink because it is refreshing and inexpensive. It is always present during a gathering of fetii, and no bringue or tamaaraa is complete without it.

The most refreshing drink of all is undoubtedly fresh coconut water. It is the cheapest drink, after tap water. However, it is important to choose young fruits, which have sweet water. Once the nut has hardened, the water turns sour.

PAPEETE MARKET

Le marché ("luh mar-SHAY"), as Papeete's market is known, is housed in a series of old warehouses. It is clean and free of unpleasant odors. Everything is available: bread, fish, meat, fruit, vegetables, coconut oil soap, tikis, and pareus. The market reflects an earlier Papeete—earthy, vibrant, colorful, and full of amiable confusion. Through a law that prohibits non-Polynesians from dealing in the produce of the soil, only Polynesians are allowed to sell fruit and vegetables. The Chinese sell other types of products.

The market is most crowded between 5 a.m. and 8 a.m. on Sunday morning. The arrival of fresh fish at 5 a.m. and 4 p.m. marks the height of activity. Most of the market stallholders come from outside Papeete, and they arrive in trucks at about 4 a.m. Many vegetable and fruit sellers come from the outer islands, and they stay in Papeete until all their stock is sold. Some stay with fetii, but most sleep in the large covered hall next to the market. In the evening, the hall is transformed into a huge municipal dormitory when everyone spreads out their mats for the night.

The market is the heart of Papeete. It is the favorite meeting place of Papeete residents and of outer islanders. Stories, gossip, and rumors all start here.

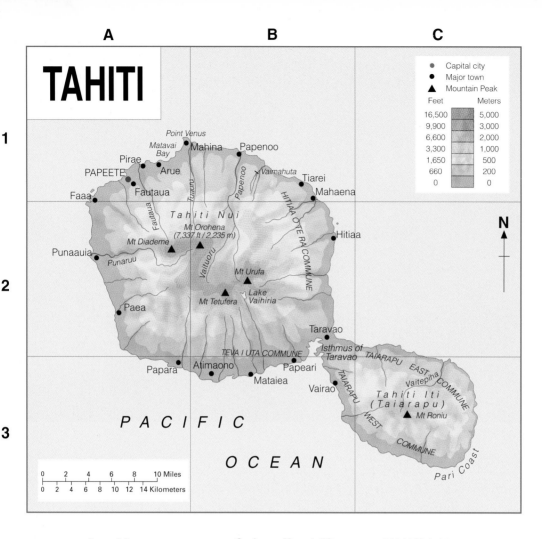

TAHITI

A   B   C

1

Point Venus
Matavai Bay
Mahina
Papenoo
Pirae
PAPEETE
Arue
Fautaua
Faaa
Vaimahuta
Tiarei
Mahaena

Tahiti Nui
Mt Orohena
(7,337 ft / 2,235 m)
Mt Diademe
Hitiaa
HITIAA O TE RA COMMUNE

2

Punaauia
Punaruu
Mt Urufa
Lake Vaihiria
Mt Tetufera
Paea

Taravao
Isthmus of Taravao
TEVA I UTA COMMUNE
Papara
Atimaono
Papeari
TAIARAPU EAST COMMUNE
Mataiea
Vairao
Vaitepiha
Tahiti Iti (Taiarapu)
TAIARAPU WEST COMMUNE
Mt Roniu

3

P A C I F I C

O C E A N

Pari Coast

Capital city
Major town
Mountain Peak

Feet	Meters
16,500	5,000
9,900	3,000
6,600	2,000
3,300	1,000
1,650	500
660	200
0	0

N

0   2   4   6   8   10 Miles
0   2   4   6   8   10   12   14 Kilometers

QUICK NOTES

OFFICIAL STATUS
Autonomous territory of France

LAND AREA
402 square miles (1,041 sq. km)
French Polynesia:
land: 1,544 square miles, 4,000 sq. km
total: 1,545,000 sq miles, 4,001,550 sq. km

POPULATION
110,000 (French Polynesia: 200,000)

CAPITAL
Papeete

COMMUNES (Associated communes)
Arue, Faaa, Hitiaa o te ra (Papenoo, Tiarei, Mahaena, Hitiaa), Mahina, Paea, Papara, Papeete, Pirae, Punaauia, Taiarapu East (Faaone, Afaaiti, Pueu, Tautira), Taiarapu West (Toahotu, Vairao, Teahupoo), Teva I Uta (Mataiea, Papeari)

LONGEST RIVER
Papenoo, 15 miles (24 km)

HIGHEST POINT
Mount Orohena, 7,337 feet (2,235 m)

AVERAGE RAINFALL
73 inches (1.85 m)

OFFICIAL LANGUAGES
French and Tahitian

MAJOR RELIGIONS
Evangelism and Roman Catholicism

NATIONAL FLOWER
Tiare Tahiti

CURRENCY
French Pacific franc (*Cour de Franc Pacifique*)
US$1 = 93 CFP

MAIN EXPORTS
Tourism, cultured pearls, and copra

MAIN IMPORTS
Food, fuel, building materials, consumer goods, and automobiles

IMPORTANT DATES
June 29 (Internal Autonomy Day)
June 29–July 14 (Heiva i Tahiti)
December 2 (Tiare Tahiti Day)

HISTORICAL FIGURES
King Pomare II, converted Tahiti to Christianity
Queen Pomare IV, sovereign who handed Tahiti
    over to the French government
Pouvanaa a Oopa, father of Tahitian nationalism

LEADERS IN THE ARTS
Ruy Juventin, painter
John Mairai, playwright
Madeleine Moua, *tamure* dancer who revived
    the traditional dancing of Tahiti
Duro Raapoto, poet and linguist

GLOSSARY

Afa Tahiti ("AH-fah tah-hih-TIH")
Children of European and Polynesian parents.

ahimaa ("ah-hee-MAH-ah")
Food baked in an underground oven.

breadfruit
A staple in the Tahitian diet; eaten boiled or grilled, the fruit has the taste and texture of bread.

bringue ("BRAING")
Party with singing, dancing and drinking.

Demis ("doh-MEE")
Descendants of early marriages between Polynesians and Europeans.

fafaru ("fah-fah-ROO")
Raw fish marinated in sea water.

fetii ("fay-tee-EE")
Relative, close friend.

himene ("hee-MAY-nay")
To sing, song; from the English word "hymn."

hombo ("HOM-boh")
Delinquent who glorifies outlaws and comic book characters.

hupe ("HOO-pay")
Mountain wind.

mahu ("mah-HOO")
Transvestite.

maraamu ("mah-rah-AH-moo")
Strong wind blowing from the southeast.

marae ("mah-RAH-ay")
Ancient place of worship.

motu ("moh-TOO")
Small island.

Popaa ("poh-pah-AH")
Foreigner, usually a French person.

popoi ("POH-poy")
Breadfruit paste eaten with coconut milk.

raau ("rah-AH-oo")
Traditional Tahitian natural remedies.

Taata Maohi ("tah-AH-tah mah-OH-hee")
Name by which Polynesian Tahitians refer to themselves; literally, "people of Polynesia."

tahua ("tah-HOO-ah")
Traditional healer.

tamaaraa ("tah-MAH-ah-RAH-ah")
Large feast of ahimaa.

tamure ("tah-MOO-ray")
Tahitian dancing.

tiki ("tee-KEE")
Carved figures representing ancient Polynesian gods.

Tinito ("tee-NEE-toh")
Chinese.

truck ("TRUCK")
Minibus used for public transport.

vahine ("vah-HEE-nay")
Woman.

BIBLIOGRAPHY

Andersen, Johannes C. *Myths and Legends of the Polynesians.* Mineola: Dover, 1995.

Heyerdahl, Thor, and F. H. Lyon. *Kon-Tiki: Across the Pacific by Raft.* Washington Program, 1995.

Howard, Michael. *Gauguin.* London: Dorling Kindersley, 1993.

Moorehead, Alan. *Fatal Impact: An Account of the Invasion of the South Pacific 1767–1840.* Mutual Publishing, 1989

Putigny, Bob. *Tahiti and Its Islands.* Singapore: Les Editions du Pacifique, 1985.

INDEX

INDEX

INDEX

PICTURE CREDITS